Rich White Folks

Rich White Folks
Growing Up Black in America

Robert H. Randolph

Outskirts Press, Inc.
Denver, Colorado

Outskirts Press, Inc.
http://www.outskirtspress.com

ISBN: 978-1-4327-5203-3

Outskirts Press and the "OP" logo are trademarks belonging to Outskirts Press, Inc.

PRINTED IN THE UNITED STATES OF AMERICA

Dedication

I dedicate this book to my five beautiful children, Alicia, Mary, Robbie, Jason and Jon, with whom I want to share what growing up was like for me. My fondest hope is that life will be much better for them and their children and that someday we can all be proud of and never forget where we came from.

In addition, this book is dedicated to Alice Bucca, my life partner, who encouraged me to keep plugging away at getting my story on paper. Alice is the person who helped with the last details of editing, for which I am eternally grateful and thankful.

Finally, this book is also dedicated to Jerilyn Bredbury. She is the person who lovingly listened to my childhood stories and suggested that I share them with others. Thank you, Jerilyn, for your loving support and for helping me to see your vision of what other people might find important.

Contents

Introduction

This book is about the phrase I heard most often from my Dad, while growing up. The phrase was: "........... like rich white folks." The complete sentence usually referred to something I was doing or not doing properly. For example, Dad would say, "Rich white folks don't use words like ain't." He might even say, "Put your shoulders back like rich white folks do."

Rich white folks were the standard by which actions, speech, manners, and dress were constantly judged. It was a long time before I was able to observe rich white folks doing all the "right" things. By the time, I was eighteen, I moved to college, away from my father's overarching influence. The major result of my four years of college was learning to think for myself. I realized that the real goal in life was to become a human being without any labels attached. I further realized that "like rich white folks" was only a simile for being bold, classy, confident, and civilized.

In any case, I hope you will have some fun reading my story. I hope that it will trigger some of your own remembrances about the standards that your parents used to keep you from becoming a social outcast. The "rich white folks" standard was especially pungent to me as a little black kid growing up during the forties and fifties. I can now thank Dad for his wise and often misunderstood guidance. When my Dad died in 1976, at the relatively young age of 67, he left me very little that was of material value. In retrospect, his legacy was much greater. Indeed he left me with true wealth -- the knowledge of how to be and function in a world with all kinds of people. I learned how to get along with everyone from the staunchest racists, to winos, to princes, without losing my own identity or sense of self-worth. I learned to discard the labels. This made it okay for me to always express my own essence, my human being-ness.

The simplistic way of looking at all of this is that buying into labels means limitations. Stripping away the labels means true freedom.

CHAPTER **1**

Up From Slavery

IT WAS SEPTEMBER 1987 in Brussels, Belgium. I was one of several International Data Corporation's (IDC's) Analysts invited to a special dinner hosted by Solomon Brothers. The dinner meeting took place in a private dining room at one of Belgium's premier restaurants. The special dinner guests were Solomon's major investment clients from all over Europe.

Starting on the opposite side of the table, each IDC analyst was to stand and give a five-minute speech on his area of computer market expertise. My colleague finished his five-minute presentation and suddenly all eyes were on me. I was the IDC Analyst responsible for tracking the products, and the marketing and business strategies of Digital Equipment Corporation. My talk would be one of the most important ones. I began my talk slowly, but determined to capture the moment with a spellbinding speech that would stay within the five-minute time limit.

"Digital is riding an interesting wave of success right now, but there are some flaws in its strategy which I will highlight over the next few minutes," I said, while glancing around the room to see the impact of this dramatic opening statement.

I knew I had scored a home run, when I sat down six minutes later and asked, "Are there any questions?" The stone cold silence told me that my mini-presentation had been so complete and clear that the audience had no questions. As I looked around the room, I remember thinking about the irony of this situation. Here I was, the first generation grandson of an African American slave from Central Texas giving a speech to some of the most prestigious, high-powered investors in Europe.

How did I get here? What events brought me to this place? How had I prepared myself to be here? There was indeed much for which to be thankful.

According to my family's oral history, my paternal grandfather was born about 1832 in Central Texas, a few miles north of the Brazos River. My grandfather's slave-master allowed him to be educated such that he was very skilled at reading, writing, and arithmetic. Ultimately, Grandpa Bob Henry -- I was named for him – worked, wheeled and dealed enough to purchase his freedom from slavery. He apparently saved enough funds to buy a 100-acre plot of land just across the road from his former owner.

The farm was halfway between the towns of Marlin, and Chilton, Texas. Today, Texas interstate Route 7 connects the two towns. Marlin, which is about thirty miles east of Waco, Texas, is the county seat of Falls County. Chilton is a very small town that was originally built around a cotton gin where all the surrounding farmers brought their cotton crops to be "ginned" -- removing the seeds from the cotton fibers.

Grandpa Bob Henry designed and built a four-room house, which is now rapidly decaying. That house on what we, in the Randolph family, refer to as the "Randolph Homestead," consisted of two bedrooms, a small kitchen, and a large dining room. There was a good-sized back porch at the back of the second bedroom. With the farm in place, Grandpa Bob Henry decided to have a family. In 1875 he married Delila Jourdan. They had ten children and prospered for some time. Because of his education and inherent intelligence, he became an advocate, or lawyer, for many of the surrounding Black families.

He probably spent a lot of time keeping his brother, we called him Uncle Archie, out of jail. You see, Uncle Archie was a notorious cattle rustler feared throughout Central Texas for his brazen looting of large cattle herds. Uncle Archie was sort of the "Speedy Gonzalez" of cattle rustlers -- now you see him and now you don't. Eventually, a determined posse of Texas Rangers and irate cattle ranchers surrounded Uncle Archie in a small log cabin. He climbed through the chimney and made a daring escape. After this close call, Uncle Archie's only choice was to flee to Eastern Canada, where he established a whole other branch of the Randolph family. However, that is another story.

Grandpa Bob Henry's first wife, Delilla, died over the course of time. Finally, at the age of seventy-seven, he married a lovely, Mexican woman named Margaret Bell. Her family still lives in Marlin, Texas. Margaret was only thirty-six when she bore a son (my Dad) in 1909. Almost eighteen months later, Grandma Margaret died during the birth of a second son. She left two young babies, my Dad, Robert Cartelyou Randolph, and Collis B. Randolph.

One of Grandpa Bob Henry's sons from his earlier marriage moved to the farm to help. This son, Benjamin Glover Randolph (I called him Uncle Glover) gradually took over the day-to-day operation of the farm. About five years later, in 1914, Grandpa Bob Henry died at the age of 82, leaving the two young orphans in the care of their older half brother and his wife. Dad's brother was a tough taskmaster. As soon as his kids (there were eleven of them) and his two orphan siblings were old enough to work, they became an integral part of the farm's workforce.

Because the pressure to make the farm sustain a large family was so intense, Dad had to leave school to do farm work full time. He only finished the third grade in his one-room country school. It made no difference that he was a bright kid or had more potential than the other kids. The survival of the farm took precedence over his formal education.

Since Grandpa Bob Henry had died reportedly of acute indigestion, Uncle Glover made a rule that no one could eat any food after 5 PM. Guests, preachers, relatives or others were included in this rule -- if you were in that house you did not eat after 5 PM. That left time for one of Uncle Glover's favorite past times -- telling stories. This usually took place on the back porch. Uncle Glover would fill his corncob pipe, lean back in an old rocker and launch into a story. Kids could sit and listen as long as they didn't say a word. This was the era when kids were better seen than heard.

Sometimes the stories were about the old days. For example, Uncle Archie's exploits were one of his favorite subjects. Sometimes he would give his analysis of a current event, like the Great War (World War I) that was raging in Europe. One evening, after reading a horrendous account of the devastating and death wielding attacks by German submarines, he launched into a story that frightened everyone within earshot.

Dad and the other kids listened with rapt attention as Uncle Glover laid out the awesome feats of the German submarines. Having heard some of Uncle Glover's stories myself, I am sure he embellished the World War I stories heavily. He probably embellished them to the point of creating the affect of the most gripping ghost story that anybody had ever heard. He evoked some very frightening images of German submarines in the fertile minds of his young audience. Here, in my Dad's own words, is the story of his first and only direct encounter with a "German submarine."

"Glover had a way of telling us news that made it so real that we started thinking that the war was going on right in the next county. He spared us no details about how the war was being waged.

German submarines were the horrific war machines that he was most fascinated with. His stories about how viscous they were, and how they were responsible for so many deaths scared us nearly to death. We often had nightmares about German submarines spewing death and destruction across Texas. We knew that there would be no escape if we ever got close to one.

Then one fateful day a strange thing happened. It was a

typical super hot day in Central Texas. It must have been at least 115° in the shade. Three of us boys had sneaked down to the pond near the center of the farm. The pond was a good place to hide out from work. As I stepped out of the pond and picked up my pants (we didn't wear shirts or shoes), I heard this terrible roaring noise in the sky. It was off in the distance, but it kept getting closer and closer and sounding louder and louder. I could see fire and smoke spewing out of this thing. As the sound got louder and louder, it hit me -- this must be a German submarine. I knew I was going to die any second. The only hope was to run for a nearby neighbor's house.

I shouted, 'German submarine, German submarine!!' to save my buddies, who were still splashing around in the pond. Then I took off running as fast as I could to the neighbor's house. I was shouting 'German submarine, German submarine!!!' As I ran for my life, I managed to get one leg in my pants so I wouldn't die naked. The thing kept coming and coming. It was almost right on top of me. I expected one of those torpedo things to hit me on top of the head any second. By the time I got to the neighbor's, I fell into their front door. I was so out of breathe that all I could do was point up at the sky and stammer. 'German Submarine, Geeerrmmann sub, sub mar, mar, German submarine!!' The neighbor, Ma Scruggs, kept asking, 'What's the matter with you boy? What's the matter with you?' I kept pointing to the sky, saying, 'Ger.......man....sub.....marine, Ger.......man....sub.....marine!' It was a whole couple of days later before I learned that I had seen my first airplane. It was a big relief to know that we wouldn't be killed by a German submarine."

At age fifteen, Dad ran away from home. He decided that he would rather take his chances out in the world than live the rest of his life as an indentured slave. Dad often told a funny story about one of his adventures while making the big escape from home. It seems that several other boys had the same idea. They ended up in a small pack headed for West Texas, where they had heard there was a lot of cotton to be picked. Eventually, an older man joined the pack and became its de facto leader. One night, during a full moon as the group moved through the woods they were stopped dead in their tracks by a huge, ferocious appearing animal transfixed in the bright moonlight. It had to be a mountain lion or perhaps even a bear. The leader took the initiative and started surreptitiously looking for a stick to chase this ferocious animal away. Each time the leader would find a stick he thought big enough to do the job, he would test it by trying to break it across his knee. Dad said that, "By the time he found a stick that was big enough, there must have been at least a cord of wood stacked in the clearing." It seems the leader had created a very large pile of wood before finding the right stick. Finally, after all of this fearful activity, the animal turned and ran away. They had just enough time to discover that the "mountain lion" or "bear" was only a large opossum.

Eventually, Dad and the group made their way to West Texas where there was plenty of cotton to pick. Dad left for the big city of Dallas, Texas, in late fall, when the cotton season was over. Dallas was where he learned about rich white folks, and where I was born.

CHAPTER **2**

Dad Escapes to the Big City

IT IS HARD to imagine what it must have been like for a fifteen-year-old, country boy to arrive in the big city of Dallas, with ten dollars in his pocket, no relatives or friends, and a third-grade education. Nevertheless, that is exactly what my Dad, Robert C. Randolph did. He was determined to get somewhere and do something with his life. To him, starving in Dallas was a much better alternative to living in virtual servitude on the family farm in Central Texas.

He wandered around Dallas, existing by doing odd jobs. He hustled to keep body and soul together until he established himself in Dallas. During the course of his wanderings, he learned to shoot craps. Gambling opened up a completely new set of possibilities for him.

After a few years in the big city, he met Henry W. Jackson. Henry, or Harry as some people called him, was a womanizer of the nth degree. His natural good looks, tall 6'2" stature, and straight black hair served him well in the pursuit of Dallas' finest womanhood. Henry was an impeccable dresser. He bought his clothes at the finest men's clothing stores in Dallas. Having been married twice -- divorced once and losing his second wife during childbirth -- Henry split his time between womanizing and being a single parent to his two children -- a daughter and a young son.

Dad probably met Henry through some mutual woman friend.

Henry's gentle, easy-going manner, which he probably inherited from his full-blooded Cherokee Indian mother, must have been what caused Dad to adopt him as a role model and a father figure. Dad and Henry spent a great deal of time together, chasing women and gambling all around Dallas.

Although Dad never mentioned it directly, I believe his friend and mentor, Henry Jackson, was the person who gave him the idea and got him the opportunity to "run on the road." "Running on the road" is an expression that older Black men used to mean having a job as a porter, cook, or other kind of helper on the railroad. For many Black men of that era, running on the road was not only a steady job, but allowed them to travel widely. They could discover vast new worlds of Black folks in all parts of the country. The job involved a few days of intense, backbreaking, continuous work. Often this period of intense manual labor ended with a day or two of rest and leisure in some exotic city like Detroit, Philadelphia, or even New York City.

Some of these roadrunners spent their leisure time drinking, chasing prostitutes, gambling or some combination of all of the above. As a young dude with no responsibilities, I am sure Dad partook of all of these pleasures of the flesh as often as possible. For Dad, running on the road was his missed high school and college education all rolled into one set of experiences. While he often boasted about only having finished the third grade, the experiences he had while running on the road made him much worldlier than the average Black man of his generation.

Educationally, he seems to have majored in gambling or, more accurately, shooting craps His minor was cooking. Not too long after his initial job as a cook's helper, Dad worked his way up to being a full-fledged member of the train's cook crew. This was the era of the dining car in the American railroad system. On most trains, the dining car was comparable to a three star restaurant. They served the most superb meals with linen tablecloths, the finest china, and silverware. These rolling restaurants were a marvelous place to learn the art of cooking fine cuisine. Dad took advantage of this chance to learn general cooking, as well as developing specialties such as baking pastries and preparing salads. Being a quick study was a strong asset that served him well in this role as an apprentice cook and throughout the rest of his life.

During a brief visit back to Dallas (home base), Dad finally managed a chance meeting with Henry Jackson's daughter. With the unusual name of Tressie, she was a very quiet, beautiful teenage girl, with light brown, silky smooth skin. She had long black hair that hung down to her shoulders. From the pictures I have seen, she had a buxom, round figure that could have swept any man off his feet. Apparently, that is what happened to my Dad. There was only one flaw to her natural beauty. Her left cornea was shattered by a rock thrown during a kid's game when she was ten years-old. She compensated for this flaw with her sweet personality. Tressie had survived not only her father's explosive, unpredictable bouts of rage, but life without a nurturing mother. Her mother died when Tressie was five, during the birth of her younger brother, Vivian.

The first meeting between my Dad, and this young woman, who would eventually be my mother, must have happened by chance. Given what I know about Henry Jackson's strong will, it is very possible that my future grandfather was not happy about his fellow roadrunner getting involved with his sweet young daughter.

From the way my mother, even fifty years later, stared off into space when someone mentioned my Dad's name, it must have been love at first sight. Tressie was just a shy sixteen-year-old high school girl and Dad was a 23-year-old man-of-the-world -- cook and gambler. The possibility of this relationship going any further than a chance meeting must have seemed extremely remote for both of them. *"Besides,"* my mother-to-be must have thought, *"Who would want to marry a countrified, teen-age girl with a sightless left eye?"*

In spite of the gulf between their worlds, Dad asked permission to court this lovely young woman. Given her strict upbringing, she was different from anyone he had ever met. Up to that point in time, his only relationships had been with "loose" women, party girls, and prostitutes. He was not accustomed to a shy woman who neither smoked nor drank. Although she never shared this information with me, I strongly suspect that she was a virgin before she married my Dad.

Dad and Tressie married about a year after their chance meeting and some very chaperoned courting. She was seventeen and he was twenty-four. He was ready to settle down. Tressie had just graduated from high school, but she was adult enough to decide to marry this handsome stranger in spite of her father's less than enthusiastic approval of the marriage. Henry was able to foresee that Dad's gambling would cause problems.

I was born nine months later on July 25, 1937 at Baylor University Hospital. We may have been a charity case, but knowing my Dad's propensity for going for a deal, it could have been the least cost alternative. There was also probably a bit of uncertainty around my birth since my original birth certificate says "boy Randolph" in the name space, indicating that not much thought had been given to a name for me. One very fortunate result was that my parents didn't succumb to the convenience of naming me Robert C. Randolph, Jr. I was named for my grandfather -- Robert Henry Randolph.

A psychic told me that Mom was delighted to have me come into the world. Just before I was born, Dad stopped running on the road, found a job as a cook, and chauffeur for some rich white folks. This was the beginning of his double life as a domestic by day and a free-wheeling, high stakes, impeccably dressed craps shooter at night.

CHAPTER **3**

Dad's Double Life

IN THE LATE 1930's, Dad wore only hand tailored suits, $30 Stacy-Adams shoes (size 11 AAA), silk underwear at $10 a pair, and a beaver cloth hat that cost about $50. He must have been a remarkable sight with his six-foot frame wrapped in the finest suiting material available and his brown beaver hat cocked on the side of his head as he threw the dice to win another big pot. This fine attire was part of the image he maintained for his double life as a hardworking cook and chauffer by day and a swashbuckling gambler by night.

In 1960 when my Dad came to Los Angeles, where I was living with my mother, her boyfriend recognized Dad from Dallas in the late 1930's. He remembered Dad's reputation as the Black community's best dressed, shrewdest gambler. According to A.C., Mom's boyfriend, "That nigger was known throughout Dallas as the best dressed nigger on the streets. And that nigger could shoot some craps."

When I was about three-years-old, Dad got a job in Grand Prairie, Texas, a little town on the outskirts of Dallas. The job was a so-called live-in situation, which meant that Mom and I were part of the package. So, we lived with our rich white folk employers. Mom did the housework, Dad was the cook and chauffeur, and I was a playmate to the rich little white kids. By then, Dad had bought a V-8 Ford to get back and forth to Dallas to continue his double life. To this day, I remember, as a three-year-old, telling everybody I saw about "My Daddy's V-8 Ford."

As part of the deal, Dad had convinced Mom that this live-in situation would allow them to save the bulk of their income to buy a house. He also promised that it was a temporary situation and that the hard work would all be worth it. Things went very well for a while. Then one day, Mom discovered that after six months of working and saving there was little or no money in their joint savings account.

Dad, sensing that times were changing because of the end of the Great Depression, decided to use the savings to make one last big gambling score. Unfortunately, he lost everything. He hoped to recoup before Mom found out, but it was too late. She was beside herself with anger. She had what could be called, "a long-suffering personality." This meant that she could put up with almost anything for a long time, but at some point, she would decide that enough was enough. Then she would explode, never to return to that set of circumstances. At that point, her stubbornness would set in and there was no turning back. She had spent six months washing, ironing, and taking care of those rich white folks and their kids on almost a 24/7 basis. Now, there was nothing to show for it. That was the last straw!

Mom packed me up and we left Grand Prairie to stay with her aunt Ruby in North Dallas. Dad must have panicked, because he had no idea about where to find us. We hid out for quite a while until my accident.

One evening my Mom sent me, at the ripe age of four, to the store across the busy street from where we were staying. I had to cross at a major intersection. I remember standing there on the corner, trying to decide which direction to go for a green light. I got very confused trying to figure it out, so I just started running across the street. A few feet from the curve, a motorcycle hit me. The wheel caught me right around the legs. My legs were badly bruised. I lay there in the street while they called an ambulance to take me to the hospital. This was all very exciting until they got me to the hospital. They checked me out and decided to keep me overnight. When they tried to put me in a crib, I raised hell. In my feisty, four-year-old way, I let it be known that; "I'm a big boy. I am not going to sleep in any crib. I have to have a 'big boy's bed'."

I must have been quite a sight, arguing with the hospital staff. Nevertheless, I did get a big boy's bed for my overnight stay in the hospital. Later, when I got home from the hospital, I overheard my Dad and Mom in a horrendous argument. Dad was furious about me, a four-year-old, being sent to the store across a busy street. Years later, I noticed that the memory of that accident had an unconscious effect on me until I was about thirty-five-years old. My legs would hurt whenever I was in a grocery store for more than ten minutes.

By now, Dad had lost the cook, chauffeur, live-in-maid job. Gambling became his primary means of support. In the face of Mom's no retreat attitude, Dad finally arrived at the conclusion that getting a divorce was the only alternative. I am sure that Mom reached the same conclusion. I suspect that through his connections with his former rich white employers, Dad got a first rate White attorney. That is the only explanation for what happened, because the divorce granted him sole custody of me. He must have made my mother look like the unfit mother of all time. I imagine that the motorcycle accident was a factor in his case.

I was shuffled around quite a bit during this period. Mom would try to hide me with one of her relatives. Then Dad would find me and stash me with his sister in Fort Worth. Then Mom would find out where I was and come to see me. Given the slightest chance, she would whisk me away for another brief stay with her relatives. At one point, Dad even sent me to the Randolph family farm in Central Texas for a brief stay with my Uncle Glover and his wife, Aunt Frankie. For many years, I thought they were my "other" grandparents.

About this same time, my maternal grandfather, Henry Jackson, whom I later came to call Granddad, began hearing about all the good, high paying jobs Blacks could get in Los Angeles, California. Granddad decided to pack up his car, his son, and a woman he had been seeing -- destination Los Angeles.

This decision proved to be a boon for Mom. She tracked me down, grabbed me and we were on our way to Los Angeles along with the crowd. Besides being furious, Dad must have been devastated. This time I was gone with no clue as to my whereabouts. He could no longer find my mother and intimidate her into giving me up. Surely, he must have heard rumors that the Jackson's were on their way to Los Angeles, but he was somehow unable to mount a search campaign that extended to California. For the moment, I was a closed chapter in his life.

Dad drifted into the arms and the bed of a seventeen-year-old party girl named Vida Zenobia Reed. Although no one ever told me about the details of their getting together, I surmised that they met as result of her wild partying. She was the complete opposite of my Mom. She was light skinned, shorter in stature and had a plump figure. She was considerably less intelligent than my Mom was. Vida was still kind of a schoolgirl, whose main interests were music, dancing and her next pack of Camel cigarettes. Maybe all of those differences were attractive to Dad at the time.

By now, Dad had become a construction worker, digging ditches and carrying hod (cement for bricklayers). When he talked about those times, there was always a sense of hopelessness, defeat, and just plain drudgery in his voice. When he had the strength, after a hard day of work, he continued his gambling life, but with a lot less gusto. Relief from this life of drudgery came when the government drafted Dad into the army in 1943.

He married Vida and shortly afterwards the army sent him to Fort Leonard Wood, Missouri. Later, she moved from Dallas to Lebanon, Missouri to be near him. Lebanon was a small town in southeast Missouri, about forty miles from the Fort. In the army, Dad became a cook again. He now had an entirely new marketplace in which to express his entrepreneurial tendencies -- the troops were hungry for action. Dad was the Sergeant Bilko of his day. He made a small fortune supplying the troops with bootleg whiskey and crap games. His nickname in the army was "Gramps." Almost anything the troops wanted they could get from Gramps, at a price. Dad's cooking skills protected his enterprises. He made a point of making sure that the White officers in charge of the Black units knew that he was the source of the great pastries that they frequently enjoyed. The Army opened up a completely new life for him and, ultimately, for me.

CHAPTER 4

Kidnapped to Los Angeles

AFTER A GRUELING car trip from Dallas, we arrived in Los Angeles. Cross-country car trips for Blacks in the early forties were, by definition, grueling. We were lucky that the white folks sold us gasoline without hiding behind some racially motivated excuses. Blacks did not stop at the Holiday Inn or the Red Roof motels that are so prevalent and accommodating to Blacks nowadays. Blacks learned not to try staying at a roadside motel or as they were called in those days, a motor court. That mentality still lingered with my Mom, more than fifty years later. She refused to stop at a motel while traveling by car, believing that she wouldn't be allowed to stay.

If the traveler knew where the Black section of town was, he might find a Black-owned motor court. Hopefully, that motel was not devoted entirely to the "hot-sheets" business of allowing hourly room rentals.

It was 1941. Granddad, Mom, Miss Eva (Granddad's woman friend), Mom's teenage brother, Vivian and I were thrilled to arrive, finally, in California -- the Promised Land.

Because of advice from friends whom he had met while running on the road and the availability of a big rental house, we put our California roots down near the corner of Fourth Street and Pico Boulevard in Santa Monica, California. In those days, there was a vacant lot directly on the corner. We were the next house over from the corner. It was an amazing place to live because we were about six blocks from the Pacific Ocean and about three blocks from California's leading wrestling emporium. What great times we had there! In the picture below, I am standing near the corner of Fourth and Pico Blvd.

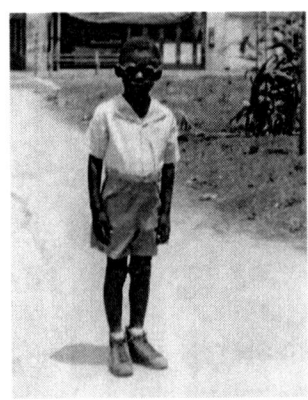

The Sidewalk Kid
Me – on the corner of 4th and Pico Blvd, in Santa Monica, CA

Mom and Miss Eva (whom I was taught to call "Mother Dear"), fanned out to find jobs as domestics (or maids). Mom did not have a chance for a job with a defense company, because of the lack of a left eye, as well as her brown skin. I doubt if she ever thought to apply at the defense plants because of a basic reticence to compete for jobs with White folks. The lessons of racism, well learned by Granddad in Dallas, said, "Don't be trying to get no White folk's job. You know you don't stand a chance of being picked over no White folks. Get a job they don't much want, like cooking, cleaning house or baby-sitting. That's how we'll beat them at their own game." Those were Grand-dad's words based on his deepest beliefs. He was the family leader who had long since bought into the racist status quo. His beliefs and attitudes prevailed.

Granddad was in good shape job-wise. He could turn his love of horses from a hobby into a full time job. He tracked down a horse stable not too far from Santa Monica. Granddad became their lead groomer, stable hand and occasional trainer. My Uncle Vivian, often dragged along to the stables, gravitated towards the fast action on the LA streets. Granddad hoped horse grooming would give his son, Vivian, some hope for a future job. Granddad kept this job for most of his working life. Even after he formally retired, the stable owner could always call him to work with the horses. Granddad often prepared horses for the Rose Bowl Parade or other big horse show events in Southern California.

Mom and I moved from Santa Monica to an apartment in Los Angeles when I was five. I became a latchkey kid with the apartment key securely attached to a chain around my neck.

That same year, I started kindergarten. I was the only Black kid in my class. We spent most of our time making art objects out of clay -- ashtrays, etc. We also did a large number of watercolor paintings. For us, hardcore subjects such as ABC's, and arithmetic were far too advanced. I met my all time best friend, in kindergarten. He was a little White kid named Robert Wilson. We liked each other because both our names were "Robert" and we both loved Captain Midnight, one of the comic book heroes of the time. Robert even took me over to his apartment to see his secret decoder ring that he got from sending in a Wheaties cereal box top. Robert W. and I were attached at the hip during the two years that I went to that school. By the time I reached first grade, I participated in such scandals as kissing little girls underneath our cots during afternoon naptime.

At Miss Eva's insistence, Granddad got a job in her employer's dinnerware manufacturing plant. Granddad worked the swing shift and kept his job at the stables as a kind of hobby. Work at the dinnerware factory was tough and Granddad started drinking cheap wine to get him through the nights. This became a problem over time.

Miss Eva's employers, the Hamiltons, were a lovely family. Tom

Hamilton owned the company called Winfield China, which made upscale California style dinnerware -- place settings, cups, bowls, etc. Later, I learned that Mrs. Hamilton was a member of the famous DuPont family. Because either Mom or Mother Dear did all of the Hamilton's cooking and housework, I was often included in the Hamilton kid's events, such as birthday parties, holiday parties, etc. Somewhere, there is a home movie with my little black face in the middle of a birthday party, eating ice cream, and cake, riding a pony and having as much fun as anyone else at the party. I thought I was a rich little white kid. It all came to a crushing halt that same December.

My grandfather became a foreman at the Winfield manufacturing plant. The Hamiltons employed my family – my grandmother, my grandfather and my mother on a part time basis. All of this dependence for employment caused my family to be intimately connected with the Hamilton's. My family was there for the births, the domestic discord, and the whole ball of wax.

Christmas day,1942, when I was five-years-old, I became painfully aware of the real gulf that existed between our two families. My Mom and I spent Christmas Eve at my grandfather's house in Venice. I woke very early and could hardly wait to get my grubby little paws on all those sparkly packages under the tree. I opened my presents, which were mostly paper because World War II was raging and everything metal was rationed or very expensive. I remember having desperately wanted a little red wagon -- a Radio Flyer as they were called. Although quite disappointed about not getting that red wagon, I played with my paper telescope, the wooden airplanes, and other modest toys I did receive.

Late morning, I went along to Brentwood, when my grandparents had to go. Mother Dear had to put the finishing touches on Christmas dinner for the Hamilton's and my grandfather went along to receive his token gift from Mr. Hamilton. When I got into their house, my "buddies" -- the Hamilton kids who were about my age -- grabbed me and pulled me into the living room to see their presents. The largest Christmas tree that I had ever seen stood in the corner of their gigantic living room. It was like stepping into an enchanted forest. There in the middle of it all was the most magnificent Lionel train set I had ever seen before or since. The train set did just about everything. The engine tooted, it stopped and loaded milk bottles at another stop it unloaded logs, then tooted again as it circled through the miniature village and pretend countryside. I even got the chance to push a few buttons at the control console. It was if I had died and gone to toy heaven.

About an hour later, it was time to go. Since there were several Hamilton kids, I had to wade through what seemed to be a sea of toys. On the way home to my grandfather's modest little house the pain and anger of being ripped from the Hamilton's magic forest turned into a white-hot rage. My little body was trembling with the loss of having to shrink back into my modest environment. The emotions of shame, combined with seething rage, so overwhelmed me, that as soon as I got to Granddad's, I went into the spare bedroom where my toys were and tore them to pieces. Hearing the commotion, my grandfather looked in the room to see what was going on. Seeing the remnants of the toys, which he had helped to buy, scattered around the room, he became enraged. He grabbed me and started violently spanking me with his belt. My mother finally intervened and we were soon on the train back to our tiny apartment in Central Los Angeles.

The pain of that incident and the frightening realization of not being rich created a Ba-humbug coloring to Christmas that has lasted for most of my life. For me, Christmas has always been associated with a sobering sense of scarcity. The air was always poignant with the stench of "not-enough." Even my most joyous Christmas' have been haunted by this underlying, unspoken pain.

Our apartment was in a multi-family unit just off 12th Street and Central Avenue. There was a lot of action in this mixed neighborhood of Blacks and Mexicans. For example, the infamous Zoot Suit riot of 1943 took place about ten blocks from where we lived. World War II was an ever-present danger. Many times during this period, there were blackouts, complete with searchlights scanning the sky for

Japanese planes. It was very eerie, especially when we actually heard airplanes flying overhead.

During the week, when Mom went to work, I was on my own. I listened to the radio a lot and ran around the neighborhood with my little Mexican friends. One day we found their parent's store of onions in their basement. For two or three days, we walked around eating large onions like apples. We thought we were so cool.

On most weekends, usually Sunday, after we moved to central LA, Mom and I would get on the "Red" car to visit Granddad in Venice. The Red car was a train that ran from downtown LA, west to Santa Monica and Venice. The old Red car tracks were in the center of Venice Boulevard and it always seemed like such a long trip.

We would have dinner at Granddad's house or we would go to the beach in Santa Monica. That is about the time that I learned to drink hard liquor. Granddad always insisted that if anyone was having a drink, I had to have one too. Even though I was only five-years-old, I learned to drink whatever anyone else was having.

Learning to drink at such an early age has served me well over the years. Alcohol has never been a taboo or a big deal. I could always take it or leave it. Some of my drinking buddies in high school (see Chapters 13-15), who discovered alcohol later in life did not fare so well. Some of them became alcoholics. Unfortunately, they never mastered alcohol.

On most of the other weekends, the movies were a kind of baby-sitter for me. I was sent to the movies, when Mom wanted to spend time with her live-in boyfriend. To this day, I retain an obsession with movies that I learned during that period of my life. Some of the special times that I remember were when my Mom took me downtown to the big, palatial movie houses. There was usually a stage show before the feature movie. That is where I first saw the Nat King Cole trio doing their 1940's hits like, "Straighten Up and Fly Right" and "Get Your Kicks on Route 66."

One night the stage show consisted of a live graveyard scene with Frankenstein defending himself against the Wolf Man. Everything was okay until the Wolf Man, and Frankenstein ran off the stage into the audience. Just as they hit the last step off the stage, every light in the theater went out and it was pitch black. I don't ever remember being so completely terrorized in my life. Shortly after that, I began having recurring nightmares about Frankenstein chasing me into the Pacific Ocean. Each time, I barely escaped.

One Saturday, a couple of my Mexican running buddies and I were on our way to a double feature starring Hopalong Cassidy, the Durango Kid, or somebody. We didn't know and didn't care. We stopped by the drug store to get some candy. Earlier that week, I had seen someone with Chiclets -- gum in a candy coated pill form. I thought they were so cute. In picking through a display at the drug store, I spotted a fancy looking blue and white checkered box that had gum in it. I grabbed that one, because the checkered box looked fancier than the Chiclets box. I bought the largest size checkered box and began chomping away at the cute gum pills inside. I was so fascinated with it. I don't think I even shared any "gum" with my buddies. This was just for me -- no sharing.

About thirty minutes into the first western feature, I had a tremendous urge to go to the bathroom. I always tried to hold on and not let that bathroom stuff interfere with a movie. But this was a very serious number two that could not be denied. I barely got to the bathroom in time. I left a thin stream of brown liquid all over the toilet. I got myself back together and got right back to the movie. I was in my chair for only five minutes when the urge hit me again. This time I didn't quite make it to the bathroom in time. I cleaned up as best I could and headed back to the movie. I barely made it back to my seat when all hell broke loose. This was hell, because the brown liquid was now oozing down my leg. With this development, I gave up and ran all the way home. It wasn't until I was about fifteen that I dared to think about Chiclets again and I discovered that I had consumed almost a full box of Feena-mint, one of the leading gentle laxatives of the 1940's and 50's.

After Mom's boyfriend was drafted, she and I moved to Venice. into a small apartment that Granddad built in his backyard garage.

I was in the second grade and walked about five blocks to school every day. One of the things Granddad taught me was that when any White folks, rich or not, called you a "nigger," your obligation to God, your Race and your manhood was to take them to fist city. I lived by that code until my Dad taught me another approach later, but for now, in Venice, California in 1944, according to Granddad, "You kick their ass good and ask no questions."

Well, it seemed that fate intervened to test my resolve. Every day as I walked to school, about three blocks from our house, two little white kids -- a little girl and a little boy -- safely ensconced behind a chain link fence, would call me a nigger. They would run back into their house as fast as they could. I would try to rip the fence down with my bare hands. I would kick and scream with all the fury I could muster. I acted out most of my horrendous rage right there on the sidewalk. I must have looked very funny. By the time I got to the schoolyard, I was fit to be tied.

I had to go right past the sandbox to get into the schoolyard. It seemed that there was always some friendly little White kid trying to get me to come over and play in the sandbox. That is where I acted out the rest of my rage. I usually punched the little kid for no apparent reason. It didn't take long to get the reputation of being the meanest little kid in the second grade. I spent a lot of time on the schoolyard bench (sitting on the bench was punishment for anti-social behavior). Each day was the same -- a morning baptismal of racism -- followed by my striking out at any face that was White and my size.

If I had not been snatched from this environment, there is no telling where I would have ended up. It is interesting to think that somewhere today, those little kids (now all grown up) are probably telling their story of this crazy little "nigger" kid they used to drive berserk every day.

CHAPTER 5

The L A Flash Takes On Lebanon Missouri

ABOUT HALF WAY through the second grade, at the age of seven, my world, and life went through a drastic Polar shift. Thanks to the American Red Cross, I had to give up my wonderful life in bright, sunny Venice, California to live with my Dad in dreary Lebanon, Missouri.

During the war, the American Red Cross performed a service of finding relatives for soldiers. Although I don't know for sure, that must have been the method my Dad used to find out where my Mom had taken me. I don't know what happened and I can only guess that some strong words or letters were exchanged. All of a sudden, my Mom got the idea to send me to live with my Dad.

One day, when Mom came home from work, she asked my thoughts about going to live with my Dad. I don't remember being thrilled with the idea; however, getting on a big choo-choo train, sounded like a great vacation. For several years, the notion of seeing my real Dad again fascinated me. For a long time, I had kept his image alive by telling everyone that the Black man on the Cream of Wheat box was my Dad. I guess I had once seen my Dad in a large white chef's hat and I just knew that guy on the Cream of Wheat box was my Dad.

My seven-year-old mind could not conceive of the possibility that this trip would somehow be permanent. By now, I had gotten used to being shuffled around, so to me this was just another one of those trips with which I was so familiar. My Mom and I had lived in five different places since she divorced Dad. I reasoned that when I was ready, I would call and have someone come pick me up and return me to Los Angeles. To me it was a thirty-day trial period. At least that was the way I heard the deal and thought it would work. Besides, it meant I was going to ride on a big "choo-choo" train. I was wildly excited about how much of an adventure a ride on a big train would be. Little did I know what was really happening. It never dawned on me that I wouldn't see Southern California again until I was sixteen years-old.

The actual exchange was like a high-level spy exchange operation. Miss Eva -- "Mother Dear" – my step grandmother arranged to take me to Dallas. The trip from Los Angeles was great. We had a sleeper that allowed us to sleep at night on the big "choo-choo" train. It was neat to crawl into the upper bunk. That was when I fell in love with trains. I don't know who paid for this trip, but it must have cost a small fortune, especially during wartime. In addition to the big exchange, the trip provided the opportunity for Mother Dear to impress her relatives with her newly acquired California prosperity. Once we were in Dallas, my new stepmother, Vida, was to take me back to Lebanon, Missouri to live with her and my Dad.

One of Vida's aunts arranged for the exchange to take place at her house in South Dallas. That aunt and the other relatives thought I was cute. They especially liked my crisp, strange California accent. It must have been quite a shock for Vida, the twenty-two-year-old party girl, to discover that she was now the parent of a bright-eyed, bushy-tailed seven-year-old. She carried it off as best she could. After a few days, Vida and I boarded the train for our triumphant journey to Lebanon, Missouri.

During this brief stay in Dallas, I saw overt discrimination for the first time. My stepmother and I went somewhere on the streetcar. In my typical fashion, I jumped on the streetcar and plopped down in the first seat I saw. I noticed the funny, little signs but, since I couldn't read, I ignored them. Suddenly, I noticed that people around me were squirming and becoming uncomfortable. I thought that was strange because I hadn't broken wind or done anything bad. While I sat there, totally confused, my stepmother grabbed me and quietly dragged me to the back of the streetcar. I couldn't figure out what I had done wrong but sensed that it had something to do with the funny, little signs. By my next trip to Dallas a few years later, I learned the stupid, senseless local customs. Black folks were somehow different from White folks. Black folks had to sit behind the signs that said, "Colored Only." If the streetcar was too crowded, the White person could simply move the signs back so that Blacks would have to give up their seats. This strange scenario thoroughly confused me. Where I had grown up, my Mexican buddies and my little White buddies were all the same. It was just a question of who had enough money to go to the movie or who the best wrestler was. This new reality was very different from any of my experiences growing up in Los Angeles. Still, I was forced to play this silly new game. That was a kind of foreshadowing of my future life in Missouri.

My stepmother and I finally arrived in Lebanon, a small town in southern Missouri near the Arkansas border. This was Dad's new home. After receiving a medical discharge from the Army because of his asthma, he needed a place to live. Why Lebanon? Dad had made a lot of money in the Army with his various "entrepreneurial" ventures (gambling, bootlegging whiskey, etc.). He needed somewhere to invest the money fast before it got away. He decided to buy land in Lebanon and settle there. The fact that this town was only forty miles from Fort Leonard Wood, meant that there was a great source of possible future business from the soldiers that moved through the Fort.

Dad bought a large triangular piece of land that was one block long on one side. He built a barbecue restaurant at the upper end of the triangle. This land and the restaurant were located on the upper end of the White community and the lower end of the Black community. Dad had set the restaurant up so that two nights a week the customers were predominantly White folks. Two other nights during the week were set aside for Black folks. One or two nights the crowd was mixed. The jukebox was set up along those same lines. There was a set of Black rhythm and blues records and another set of "hillbilly" records. The most popular R&B song was "Caldonia" and the most popular hillbilly song was "Smoke on the Water and The Land and the Sea."

My life was totally different from what I had known in Southern California. It was very cold, there was no indoor plumbing and I stood out from the other black kids like a sore thumb. School was very different too. I had gotten rid of the two little White kids that called me nigger every morning. They were replaced with a bunch of Black kids that called me nigger. I was confused. I had not gotten any training about what to do when Black kids called me nigger, especially when they were much bigger than I was. Since I was only in the second grade, it seemed that everybody was bigger than I was.

My new school was a one-room school, with grades from one to eight, for "colored" only. Miss Briggans taught all eight grades every day. She would start with the first graders. There might be three or four of them in any given year. Then she would work her way up to the eighth graders by late afternoon. Some years we didn't have eighth graders and some years we didn't have first graders. There was a second large room set aside for high school, when there were enough kids for high school. The second year in high school seemed to be the time when most of the kids dropped out anyway.

An old semi-retired man, Professor Williams, taught high school. He could be easily activated or deactivated depending on the need for a high school teacher. Later, when Lebanon's Black population expanded, the White school board hired a full time teacher for the "colored" high school.

Although I didn't realize it at the time, this one room school was the best thing that ever happened to me. When I arrived in Lebanon, I was a perfect victim of California's experimental school system. I did not know my ABC's. I could not read and I had never heard of such strange things as multiplication tables. On the other hand, I was a whiz with clay, crayons, and watercolors. I often filled up a Big

Chief tablet (they were a nickel then) with page after page of tight little drawings. They were always various kinds of airplanes locked in aerial dogfights. They were either German fighter planes or Japanese planes attacking or being attacked by American fighter planes. During my stay in the modern California school system, learning my ABC's seemed too complex for human comprehension and things like arithmetic and multiplication tables were only for the gifted. I remember a little girl in my kindergarten class that could read a newspaper. My friends and I would worship at her feet. To us she was a goddess. We fell dumb with awe whenever she stood up and read something in class. Reading was a far off dream for us. On the other hand, if it never happened for us, we could fall back on our artistic skills.

It wasn't long before my Dad and Miss Briggans realized that I had a lot of catching up to do. I think they made a deal not to put me back in the first grade but to hold me in the second grade if there wasn't some drastic improvement. This was probably that point in my life when I escaped the label of "slow" or a special needs kid.

Dad took on the task of bringing me up to speed. The result was that my new life acquired another level of misery. Every morning, during breakfast, I had to learn and recite from memory, the multiplication tables up to 12 x 12. I started at one-times-one equals-one and eventually got up to twelve-times-twelve equals one hundred forty four. I learned my ABC's from the first graders as they learned them. I remember being so proud when I was finally able to recite my ABC's. Armed with this advanced knowledge of my ABC's, I was ready for a daily grilling about reading. Dad was determined to bring my far-off dream into present reality as soon as possible. Although he had only finished the third grade, he didn't want an academically-challenged son.

Dick, Jane and Spot became my new breakfast companions. I got very tired and frustrated "seeing Dick run" and of "seeing Dick and Jane run." While Dick and Jane were running all over the place, Spot (their dog) would jump. However, my Dad hung in there and made sure that I took Dick, Jane and Spot through their paces every morning. He threatened that if I didn't get smarter, I would end up like "Little Black Sambo" another racial straw man of the forties.

To his credit, Dad never seemed to tire of the monotony of our breakfast ritual. Given my anger about the breakfast ritual, I might have regressed to my former habit of going to school and beating up the first little kid I saw, but that was impossible. All the kids seemed to be much bigger than I was. Besides, they were all cousins and if you messed with one of them, you had to beat up a whole family. In addition, there were no weak little White kids to take vengeance on as I had done when I lived in Venice. Therefore, I had to live with my pent up emotions.

CHAPTER 6

The City Kid Goes Country

TO THIS DAY, it is a wonder that I can still eat breakfast. A daily grilling about either arithmetic or reading accompanied my early breakfast life. The daily grilling started with the multiplication tables. I had to recite them before I could eat or, if I were lucky, I would get to recite them after I ate. Later, I had to recite my ABCs or read a passage from Dick and Jane. Then I was off to school.

On a typical day in this one-room school, Miss Briggans, our teacher, would work with each grade; give them an assignment and move on to the next grade. She worked her way from the first grade to the eighth grade every day. At recess, we would play softball. Everybody was encouraged to play no matter how small he or she was or how rotten he or she played. I was fortunate that I was almost a natural at softball. Ultimately, that is what got me accepted into the "in" group. Although I was a skinny kid, I was strong enough to hit long balls. I loved softball because it gave me a chance to show what I could do. It was usually the boys against the girls.

The girls had a big person -- Lula Mae -- that they could rally around and coincidentally, the boys had a big person -- Lebert -- that we could rally around. Sometimes, if Miss Briggans had a particularly trying day, she would let us out for the afternoon recess and we would stay out the rest of the afternoon, until school was out.

Miss Briggans had come to Lebanon from a small town in Kansas called Coffeyville. It must have been difficult for a young Black woman graduating with a BA in Education in the late thirties, to find a bona fide teaching job. I am sure that she had trouble in her state, Kansas, since it had a very confused point-of-view about segregation. In some parts of Kansas, there were signs for "Colored" and "White" entrances to restaurants. While, in other parts of the state, there were fully integrated schools. Topeka, Kansas was the city in which the famous 1954 school desegregation case originated.

Miss Briggans must have had a distant relative who lived in Lebanon, who encouraged her to take the teaching job there. Miss Briggans was a handsome woman, just a little on the plump side, weight wise. She had a soft-featured face and beautiful, smooth, chocolate brown skin without any blemishes. Her large, round bottom was one of her most prominent features. Her large booty would jiggle as she wove her way among the rows of desks, especially when she didn't wear a girdle. It is rather easy to see why the town's most eligible bachelor, Adolph Meacham, married Miss Briggans a few years after I came to Lebanon.

Miss Briggans was an incredible woman who was totally committed to seeing that we had a well-rounded school experience. She created all kinds of extra-curricula activities. These activities included school plays, Halloween parties, and Christmas parties. To keep things interesting, she would sometimes do crafts. For example, one time she had us collect sawdust from our woodpiles and we made sawdust (and flour) bowls. Sometimes, if we each brought 25 cents, Miss Briggans would make a big pot of chili for lunch.

The fact that most of the students were related to each other was another Lebanon phenomenon. Most of them were first, second or third cousins. I was definitely an outsider. I was not related to anyone. My clothes were very different. My speech was quite weird and my father was the leading businessman in the Black community. In spite of all these ingredients for being a social outcast, I worked extra hard at belonging. My strategy was simple. I would be smarter and stronger than anyone. My major goal was to play softball better than anyone. Then I could belong. This strategy had worked with my little Mexican friends in Los Angeles and therefore it had to work with these country folks in Lebanon.

Aside from my burning desire to belong at school, I had the additional problem of having to live with my stepmother. Remember, she was the party girl turned instant mother. She was an unhappy "camper" and often took it out on me. At least from my point of view, it seemed that she did many little things to make my life miserable. For example, because my feet were growing so fast, she insisted that I go barefoot all summer. It wasn't too bad until I had to go downtown to a movie while not wearing shoes. I felt as though all of those White people were staring at my bare feet. This was one of the most embarrassing periods of my life.

When it became apparent that I would do anything to avoid going to our outdoor toilet, she started giving me castor oil almost daily. The worst time was when she gave me castor oil on my birthday. I remember pleading with her to give it to me on any other day, but not my birthday. She gave me a big dose of castor oil anyway. Birthdays were never the same again.

The only indoor plumbing consisted of a water faucet that piped city water into our house. We had to wash clothes with a "scrub" board -- a rectangular device with a raised, corrugated tin surface on one side. Washing clothes consisted of dipping them into warm soapy water (usually in a large tin tub) and rubbing them hard against the rough surface of the scrub board until they seemed clean.

Taking a bath was not too different from washing clothes. The summers were not too bad, but bathing in the winter was a painful experience. First, a hot fire had to be made in the wood burning stove that served as central heating. Then a large pot of warm water was poured into the large tin tub used for washing clothes. The tub was then pulled up as close as possible to the warm stove.

I first learned about the "goose flesh" phenomenon during one of those bathing episodes. You had to wet and soap one side of your body that was closest to the warm stove. After rinsing that side, you turned around and quickly washed the other side. If you weren't fast enough, the wet side away from the heat became a massive sea of goose flesh. All of this took a while to get used to. I hated it. The memory of a warm bathtub with hot and cold running water soon faded far into my distant past.

Long underwear in the winter was another unwelcome indignity that came with living in Lebanon. During my first winter there, my stepmother introduced me to long underwear. After getting accustomed to the itching all over my body, caused by the rough wool against my skin, I had to learn how to deal effectively with the "trap door" at the back of the union suit. Since I was taking laxatives most of the time, quick access (or not quick enough access) to the trap door was a terrifying challenge. Sometimes, I just didn't make it in time. When that happened, I was in for a very long day. High cost was the other problem with long underwear. This meant I could only have one extra pair. Therefore, if the spare pair didn't get washed, then I had to wear the ones I had on for days or maybe weeks. There was some kind of rule that once you started wearing long underwear in November, you would catch pneumonia if you switched back to short underwear before late spring. Long underwear was like Daylight Savings time that only came at certain times of the year.

Life went on this way until one day; my Dad's entrepreneurial empire suddenly fell apart.

CHAPTER **7**

King Bob's Empire Crumbles

IT WAS ABOUT 1945 when my Dad's business empire crumbled. By then, I had survived my entry into life in Lebanon. I had learned my multiplication tables up to the twelve's (twelve times twelve is one hundred forty-four) and was shakily reading long passages of "Dick and Jane" with only a few corrections. Life was moving along rather smoothly, when Dad decided to expand his business. That bad decision is what caused his empire to crumble a short time later.

In those days, Missouri state law prohibited the sale of any kind of liquor on Sundays. Mindful of this law as well as the enormous profit potential, Dad could not resist the temptation. He bought a house directly across from the barbecue place. A White couple lived there and they were probably happy to get away from this noisy neighborhood with all kinds of cars driving up and down their quiet street until restaurant closing time.

On Sundays, Dad spread army blankets on the floors and stocked the kitchen with tubs of cold beer. Somehow, he got the word spread to the Black troops stationed at Fort Leonard Wood and they flocked to this house in Lebanon where they could drink beer and shoot craps all day Sunday. This was the beginning of the end.

Either hostile neighbors or uninvited town locals, blew the whistle on Dad's illicit operation. In order to stay out of jail, Dad had to sell everything except the small house where we lived. His White, uptown lawyer friend was very effective in helping with the liquidation. Who knows, maybe there was some kind of conspiracy "to stop that nigger from buying too much land." Eventually, we had to sell the small house where we lived. We moved from there down the block into what was once the gambling house. The Barbecue place closed and was sold. It had been the first to go. Somehow, Dad managed to save enough money to buy a truck. He roamed around the Missouri countryside hauling wood, corn or anything he could to make money. I sometimes went with him to do my share. Eventually we had to move out of the gambling house, when it too had to be sold. The only place we could go was to move in with one of Dad's erstwhile partners -- William "Bill" Cooper. Bill and his wife, Lucille, had five children -- three boys and two girls. We moved into their small three-bedroom house. I slept on the floor in the boys' bedroom. Margery, one of the Cooper girls was about my age. I spent a lot of time trying to get her to snuggle under my blanket to play "doctor" when our parents weren't looking. Somehow, her little brothers knew what was going on, and they did their best to thwart my attempts at playing "doctor" with their sister. In a few months, Bill and Lucille decided to move back to Galveston, Texas where they were born. We had to move again.

Thankfully, Dad had made enough money from the trucking business to rent a large building. The building was a long rectangular structure with a galvanized metal exterior. There was enough room to create a grocery store in the front end with enough room for living quarters in the back end. We moved from the Cooper's house into the store.

Not being the kind of businessman to be swayed by market research, Dad decided there would be enough customers to support a second grocery store in this neighborhood. Therefore, we began stocking the shelves with groceries.

When Dad got an idea, he went with it no matter what. Somehow, he took no notice of the fact that a White-owned, well-established grocery store was on the opposite corner. That store, I can't remember the name -- let's call it Sam's -- had been there for twenty or thirty years. Sam's had become a kind of cornerstone in the Black community. Credit accounts were its main offering. Any Black family that was down on its luck could go into Sam's, and get a bag of groceries by signing the credit book. That was Sam's major competitive advantage. It became a major hurdle for the success of our grocery store.

It took a while for us to build up a grocery inventory that could compete with Sam's. The first few months of operation were a real struggle. One day, about three months after we opened, Dad got an idea for a competitive breakthrough. He decided to offer fresh pork meat that was better than anything that Sam's could offer.

Not being the kind of entrepreneur that took the easy road, Dad purchased a huge glass-enclosed meat case and had it shipped from Texas. Even though it took a long time to get to Lebanon, the shiny glass-fronted case was going to insure our ability to compete with Sam's. The meat case deal included a washing machine, which broke down shortly after it arrived. Undaunted, my stepmother used the rollers on the machine to wring out clothes after washing them by hand. Even that was a big improvement over the manual system.

Seizing on the fresh pork meat as our new competitive edge, Dad used his contacts with farmers that had supplied him black market meat during the war years. Just as he did during the war, he went out to the farms, slaughtered and butchered hogs on the spot. He advertised widely in the Black community that our meat came directly from the farm, and not from some meat packing plant in Chicago. We began stocking fresh-killed pork. My stepmother made laundry soap from the extra fat trimmed from the hogs Dad brought home for the meat case. For a brief period, it seemed that the store would be a success and Bob Randolph, the ex-Barbecue-man, now Bob the grocery man, would make a comeback.

This was about the time my "rich white folks" lessons began. For example, one day I said, "I ain't going to play with those kids anymore." Dad heard me. He looked at me with a stern face and said, "rich white folks don't use words like ain't." At first, I thought he was kidding. Then I realized that he was serious. So, I never used the word "ain't" in a sentence again. Since, during my early years in California, I had spent a great deal of time with rich white folks, I could easily relate to his point of view.

My lessons based on the "rich white folks" standard continued until I was about fifteen. One day Dad said something about "rich white folks" and I laughed. It just struck me as funny. There were a few nervous moments until Dad got the joke of that phrase. Then he, too, laughed. Although he never admitted it, I think in that instant he knew that I would be okay -- that I would at least have a feeling for the simile he was speaking about. I think he knew that I would have some sense of the style, the class, the responsibility, the self-confidence, etc., that he had observed from his narrow experience with "rich white folks."

For several months, although I was unaware of it, Dad placed himself at the center of a major Lebanon controversy. The all-White, Lebanon School Board had to do something about the decrepit, "colored only," one-room school building which was literally falling down. The school board suggested that the old school be torn down and that all the Black kids be moved to an old abandoned building, which had been a USO Center during the war. This huge USO building was built in the center of the Black community to make sure that none of the Black soldiers from Fort Leonard Wood ever ventured into downtown Lebanon for entertainment. The soldiers had to make do with the entertainment found in the USO building surrounded by Lebanon's Black folks.

My Dad had the audacity to suggest, through various channels, including his White attorney, who was part of the downtown establishment, that there were some other alternatives. Dad had the gall to suggest that it might be better to build a new school for Blacks. Dad even went so far as to suggest that, given the small number of Black children, it might be more economical to integrate the schools. I don't think Dad knew that the Missouri State Constitution specifically forbade Black children from being educated in the same school with

White children -- "the races must receive separate but equal education." A key section of the Missouri State Constitution, stipulated that, "No white child shall be taught in the same public school classroom with a Negro child." The State Constitution was worded that way or words to that effect.

Traditionally, Lebanon's Blacks had operated with a kind of slave mentality. They were happy with anything the White folks gave them and they would simply accept it without question and say, "Thank you, thank you Massa."

With his uppity attitude, Dad, an "outsider," had created a seething cauldron of resentment and hostility in the Black community. One night, all of that hostility boiled over into the front yard of our grocery store. A large number of the town's Blacks formed a boisterous protest mob to show their anger against Dad's outspoken challenge to the Lebanon School Board. This near riot took place, coincidentally, directly across from the USO building across the street from our store.

The crowd was yelling and inviting Dad to step out of the store. One loud voice said, "Come on out here Nigger!"

I don't think I ever saw my Dad so calm and collected as he stood in the narrow doorway of the grocery store, he shouted back, "I am not going anywhere. You folks need to go home."

Another loud voice in the crowd said, "Nigger, we don't like your uppity attitude. You don't belong in Lebanon anyway!"

"I belong here just as much as anybody else." As he shouted this back at the crowd, he reached behind him and my stepmother put his 30-caliber army carbine in his hands. When he turned around, he cocked the rifle to put a bullet in the chamber. That sound sent a brief shudder through the crowd. My stepmother was standing right next to him with the huge Smith and Wesson 45-caliber revolver, which occasionally had been used to restore order in the barbecue place. She rather casually let the crowd see it too.

I was standing right behind them trying to figure out what was going on. Finally, after a long pregnant silence, it became clear that no one was willing to take the first step to heaven, and the mob quietly drifted away. As you can imagine, the grocery business fell off dramatically after that confrontation. Lebanon's Blacks staged a subtle, yet effective, boycott against our grocery store. That was the end of our grocery business. We had to move again.

CHAPTER 8

King Bob, Exiled to Kansas City

IT WAS 1946 and we had to make another new start. We moved to a small rented house on a side street about three blocks from where the grocery store had been. The two-bedroom place had a multi-colored slate rock exterior that made it look like a large, square pinto pony. It was distinct from other houses in town. The awful outdoor toilet was its main drawback. Not only was the outhouse about to crumble, but a narrow path through a sort of reed grass that was about three feet tall was the only way to reach it. Every time I went to that toilet, which was as seldom as possible, I was afraid a gigantic snake would devour me. Although no one seemed to care, I regressed to my previous life of chronic constipation.

While living in this house, I had my first gruesome assignment to kill our Thanksgiving turkey by chopping off its head with an axe. I had often watched Dad slaughter animals before, but I was in a state of shock when he asked me to kill the turkey. I guess Dad saw this event as my rite of passage to manhood, even though I was only nine years old. Anyway, I was so concerned about the turkey's feelings that I almost cut off my own foot. Both the turkey and I got through this coming of age experience. I guess it made me more of a man and allowed the turkey to fulfill its destiny.

A month later, Dad left and went to Kansas City to find work. Since there was absolutely nothing for him to do in Lebanon, he had to do something drastic. His entrepreneurial ship had sailed and there was no dry land in sight. I guess Dad chose Kansas City because he had an older brother living there. That made Kansas City a more logical choice even though Lebanon was closer to St. Louis geographically.

Dad came home from Kansas City for Christmas and did the strangest thing. All during my stay with Dad and my stepmother, we had never gone to church. On Christmas Eve, Dad insisted, almost demanded that I go to a nearby church. I was frightened. What would the people think or say to me? Most of the people there were relatives and I would stick out like a sore thumb. In spite of my fear and foreboding, I dragged myself to church based on the promise of candy from Santa Claus. Sitting there in the back of the church, I don't think I had ever felt more alone and out of place. I was ready to bolt at the slightest chance.

Then as if the Red Sea had parted, someone called my name. "Robert Randolph? Is Robert Randolph here?" the voice said.

I very sheepishly raised my hand and said, "I am Robert Randolph." I was expecting to be ushered out of church for not being a member or some other infraction.

"Would you come up and stand by the Christmas tree?" Said the minister or whoever he was.

"Yes!" I shouted as I made my way through the church, to stand next to the gigantic Christmas tree, which had all kinds of presents under it.

"There's a present here for you Robert." The voice said.

"For me?" I could hardly believe my ears as my eyes began searching for something that might have my name on it.

"Go over to that bicycle and see whose name is on it." The minister commanded.

To my surprise and glee, the tag on the bright, shiny, red bicycle said "To Robert Randolph." I was speechless as everyone in the church clapped their hands. I stood there in total shock and disbelief. I had to read it again, "To Robert Randolph." It was really true. I put my hands on the handlebars and everything from that moment on was a blur. I barely remember Santa Claus passing out candy to all the kids, but the thrill of struggling down the steps of the church with my new bike is one of my fondest memories. It almost made up for the Lionel train set experience. Since I didn't know how to ride it, I had to walk it the entire five blocks to my house.

When I got home, my Dad was grinning from ear to ear. I ran up and gave him a big hug.

This was the best Christmas present of my life. It brought back memories of the Christmases at the home of the Hamilton's when I was five or six in Los Angeles. Even though it wasn't a complete Lionel Train set, my Red Flyer bike was ten times as big and a hundred times more beautiful to me.

Dad had somehow set up the whole event at the church and he seemed as thrilled as I was. My next major challenge was to learn how to ride the darned thing. Because it was winter, I had to store my bike in my mom and Dad's bedroom. That was the only room, big enough for me to get on and coast the bike from one corner of the room to the next.

After Christmas, Dad went back to Kansas City. My stepmother and I stayed in Lebanon. Six months later, my stepmother, and I joined Dad in Kansas City. We stayed in an upstairs apartment at 15th Street (now Truman Road) and Indiana Avenue. A member of the famous Kansas City Monarchs, a Negro League baseball team, owned the house. I even had a chance to sit in the dugout during one or two K. C. Monarch's games. That was a great thrill for a kid.

By now, I was ten and in the fourth grade. This was my first experience in a segregated, big city school.

The fourth and fifth grades were in the same room. One teacher taught both grades. I was one of the academic stars of the fourth grade. My one-room school experience in Lebanon had turned me into a walking encyclopedia. I was full of facts up to the eighth grade level. My habit, of rushing through my assignment and then listening to all the other grades, paid off. I had absorbed a great deal of information.

In my new school, I had one real buddy. His name was Alvin Kelly. He was the other fourth grade academic star. We competed for top honors in our class. Alvin and I developed a camaraderie based on our friendly competition to be at the top of the class. This camaraderie lasted through the eighth grade after which Alvin joined the Lincoln High School band (Charlie Parker's Alma Mater) and we lost our connection.

One day, my Dad looked at me and said, "You are too scrawny, we have to do something about that. You are not eating right." I was ten-years-old. At that point, instead of shoving some chewable vitamins at me, he took over my diet. Deciding that I needed more protein and more green leafy vegetables, he established a new eating regimen for me.

His answer was to decree that I had to drink at least one full quart of milk a day. Sometimes, just for fun, I would put a raw egg in the milk. In addition, he scoured Safeway stores in White neighborhoods to find the very best lean ground beef. Every evening he would prepare a half-pound patty flavored with Worcestershire Sauce and A1 Sauce. To add to the meal, he would cut a head of lettuce in quarters and give me a quarter slice with Thousand Island dressing. He would sit with me as I ate to make sure I finished everything. I don't remember my stepmother getting home from work in time to join in this nightly ritual.

There is something special about knowing that your Dad is going out of his way to make sure that you grow up big and strong. No, I didn't grow up hating ground meat patties and lettuce or even Thousand Island dressing. To the contrary, I love ground meat patties and have learned my Father's way of fixing them. Each time I take a bite out of a ground meat patty, I am reminded of the great love that my father expressed for me by personally preparing my meals. It brings his love present each time.

About that same time, in 1947, my Mom came to visit from Los Angeles. At first, I was confused. I thought she had come to take me away from all of this Missouri madness. I think my Dad suspected the same thing. There were some very tense moments. I got the hint from my Dad that at some point, I would end up locked in the bathroom until she left. Although the situation didn't end up that way, it came very close to turning quite ugly. Mom finally left after a few stressful days, and my hopes of ever getting back to Los Angeles went with her.

Not long after that, on a warm Spring Sunday afternoon, Dad took me to Kansas City's Swope Park Zoo. It was a long distance from where we lived and we had to take two different streetcars. When we transferred to the second streetcar on the main line to Swope Park, it was very crowded. I pushed through the crowd looking for a seat. Dad was right behind me. I stopped and stood near two little White kids in a seat. Their parents were sitting right behind them. One of the little kids stood up on the seat to look out the window leaving a big chunk of the seat available. After a minute or so of seeing this empty space, I plopped down. The mother reached over and started to push me out of the seat. Dad appeared from out of nowhere just as this was happening. He touched my shoulder to reassure me and help me stand up. As he did that, he spoke out in a very loud voice so that everyone on the streetcar could hear him. "Son, remember I was trying to tell you what a "nigger" is? He said. "Well, that lady is a nigger!! She is messing up. Take a good look, because that's what a "nigger" looks and acts like." The mother and father sitting right next to her, turned several shades of purple. But neither one of them got up nor said a word. They must have seen the fiery rage radiating out of my Dad's eyes. They must have decided that they were not going to mess with this crazy Black man and his little kid.

At the beginning of summer, one of her relatives died and my stepmother took off with me to Dallas. Dad drove down in his truck a couple of weeks later. There was some kind of big argument between her and Dad. He threw me into the truck and we took off. Meandering around until we ended up in an East Texas town called Marshal, Texas we rented a room from an old man. The old man got up every morning at dawn and went into the pinewoods that surrounded Marshal. With a very sharp ax, the old man cut railroad crossties by hand. Dad got a job hauling these hand-hewn crossties to the yard, where they applied creosote so railroad companies could use them.

During our first two weeks in Marshal, I had my first experience of being hungry. It took about two weeks before Dad got paid. Things started to get bad and then worse. For several days, we had to eat ho-cake (a water and flour mixture cooked in a skillet) with white gravy made from flour and water. I had only one meal a day, in the evening when Dad came home -- that is, before the flour ran out. When the flour ran out, we had two or three days of eating nothing.

These lean days were in stark contrast to the previous year in Kansas City, when Dad, feeling that I was too skinny created a project to fatten me up. In a way, this East Texas camp-out was kind of fun. My Dad and I were roughing it together. For the first time, we discovered that we didn't really need the party girl.

When the crosstie hauling business dried up, Dad and I would get in the truck and drive through the countryside. When he spotted a farm that had broken down farm equipment, we would stop. Dad would offer to remove the broken down equipment free of charge. If the farmer were more astute, Dad would offer him a small amount of cash for the equipment. Many times, for lunch, Dad would buy a watermelon from a farmer and we would sit on the farmer's front porch and eat it. Sometimes the watermelon would be the price we charged the farmer for "cleaning up" his old eyesore equipment. Then we would take the machinery to a scrap iron place across the border in Shreveport, Louisiana. For a month or so, we lived this kind of gypsy lifestyle.

Then, somehow, Dad patched it up with my stepmother. We moved into an apartment when she joined us. About that time, Dad came up with a new scheme for making money. On Saturday nights, he would buy two or three cases of assorted sodas, several loaves of bread, and several pounds of fish, from the local grocery store. He would stay up most of the night deep-frying the fish and icing the soda. Early on Sunday mornings, he and I would load up everything and drive out along the back roads to find a Black, country church. Timing it so we got there just before church was over, we would set up in the church parking lot. Our little fish sandwich and soda pop concession stand off the back of the truck was nondenominational -- Baptists were as welcome as Methodists.

That was how we lived for the rest of that summer. We collected scrap iron during the week and operated the mobile fish restaurant on Sundays. At the end of the summer, Dad decided that we had to move back to Kansas City, because he felt the schools in East Texas were not good enough for my education.

CHAPTER 9

A Second and Final Exile to Kansas City

WHEN WE GOT back to Kansas City, we moved to a new neighborhood, where I completed the last half of the fifth grade at Booker T. Washington Grade School. After school was out for the summer, my stepmother and I moved back to Lebanon.

After Dad moved us back to Lebanon, he went back to Kansas City to find work. I haven't a clue why we moved back to Lebanon. I guess it was a matter of economics. Dad could live cheaply and work in Kansas City while my stepmother and I could live more cheaply in Lebanon. I started the sixth grade in Lebanon. By now, the refurbished USO building replaced the old wooden, one-room school. There was a new, full time high school teacher, a Mr. Palmer, as well as a separate part of the building devoted to high school classes. Miss Briggins still taught the elementary grades. There was also a big gymnasium, where the entire school played during bad weather. This was quite an upgrade from the old one room school. My sixth grade stay in Lebanon was a bit more luxurious.

During the summer, when the school term in Lebanon was over, my Uncle Morton, who lived in Kansas City, had me come back to Kansas City. From there he took me on a whirlwind train tour visiting our relatives. We started with relatives in Oklahoma and ended up at the Randolph Homestead in Central Texas. We would get on the train and go to a town where there was a relative. We would spend a day or two and then go on to the next relative's town. Starting in Sapulpa, Oklahoma (near Tulsa) where we visited some cousins, we went to Fort Lawton, Oklahoma to visit Uncle Morton's older sister (my aunt Eva). From there, we went to Fort Worth, Texas to visit my Aunt Josie Baker and her husband. Other than my first experience with television, the two things I remember most about that visit was the peach cobbler and the fantastic coconut layer cake Aunt Josie made for us. She was an incredible cook.

My Aunt introduced me to my cousin when I first arrived in Fort Worth. He was about three years older than I was. His job was to show me around while the adults went off and did their thing. We got together with my cousin's friends and went to one of their houses. This was the first time I ever saw a TV set, up close. There was not enough space in their tiny living room for the group of us to sit inside. We had to sit outside the living room window and watch the small TV set.

It was the summer of 1948. In the early days of TV, they only broadcasted a few shows between the hours of 6:00 AM and midnight. At midnight, the stations signed off with the Star Spangled Banner. After signing off, the stations put a graphic on the screen called a "test pattern." While the few shows that were on were interesting, after they went off, we were happy just to watch the test pattern, hoping to see something change. It never did, but it was enough for us kids to brag to everyone in the neighborhood that we had seen a real TV. In those days, seeing television was a rare and heady experience.

During the two days my uncle and I stayed in Fort Worth, my cousin told me about a very sad occurrence. The day we had arrived, one of my cousin's high school friends was buried. It seems he had been the victim of a love triangle. He had made the mistake of going out with another guy's girl. The jealous boyfriend shot the poor kid. Since I had never actually dated a girl, it was very difficult for me to understand how serious this situation was. It did leave me with the distinct impression that I didn't want to live in Texas where guys shoot each other over girlfriends.

From Fort Worth, we went to visit my cousin Myrtle in Waco, Texas. From there my Uncle and I took the final leg of our journey to our family's homestead near Marlin, Texas. Uncle Morton had been a Pullman porter and this nomadic train trip was a wonderful reminder to him of his early life. It was also his last train trip. Sadly, he died the following summer.

When this exciting summer was over, instead of going back to Lebanon, I went back to Kansas City, where my parents had moved again. We lived on 14th and Park just around the corner from where Charlie Parker, the jazz musician, had grown up. I went back to Benjamin Banneker school for the seventh grade.

That was the year that I first became acquainted with nudist colony magazines in the boy's bathroom. While I had seen some nude African women in National Geographic, the nudist magazine women looked like regular women I had seen on regular streets. We had only imagined these women with no clothes and the nudist magazines left nothing to the imagination. We sometimes fantasized about seeing our teacher, Mrs. Briscoe, who was an incredibly beautiful, light-skinned woman with brown curly hair, in one of those magazines. It was a short step from those magazines that you'd only glance at sideways, because of their forbidden nature, to "Tijuana Bibles" -- the little porno cartoons featuring movie stars and regular cartoon characters doing naughty things. I made the stupid mistake of taking a Tijuana Bible home, and having the tar beat out of me, because I refused to let my stepmother see it before I threw it away.

I was pleasantly surprised to see that some people remembered me from when I had been at Benjamin Banneker in the fifth grade. Not having to make many new friends gave me a warm feeling.

For the second time I fell madly in love with a girl. This time her name was Doris Woods. Before, in the sixth grade in Lebanon, I had fallen in love with Ernestine. She was in high school and a few years older, but that did not cool my ardor. I thought I could handle her, given the chance. The thing that both of my love objects had in common was that they didn't know I existed. However, I didn't let that fact get in my way. I spent many nights dreaming about Ernestine. If I had been old enough, she might have been the source of some pleasant nocturnal emissions. After my unrequited affair with Ernestine, I felt like a well-traveled man-of-the-world. Conquering Doris Woods, the new girl, seemed like it was only a matter of time.

Everything about Doris was perfect. She was tall, slim and had an angelic face. My one-sided romance became so intense that I started drawing comic strips every day. I would project into the future all kinds of fantastic happenings. Doris was always the brave hero and I would be watching from the sidelines. When I got to school, I was too shy to give the comic strips directly to Doris, but I made sure her closest friend got a copy.

This was about the same time that I discovered the concept of the "Equal Opportunity Role Model." I didn't know much about role models and certainly, no one told me that the role model had to look like me and had to have the same cultural background as me. The ever-present "rich white folks," who had been my background role model for many years, probably prompted this attitude. Whatever the reason, I was about twelve years old when I read about two people that became my heroes and role models for the rest of my life.

While thumbing through an encyclopedia one day, I stumbled across an article about Leonardo Da Vinci. As I read about him, I remember being fascinated by the diversity of his knowledge and his activities ranging across art, science and engineering to architecture. As I read more and more about Da Vinci, I became convinced that he was the kind of person I wanted to be when I grew up. This was the beginning of my "Leonardo Da Vinci complex." Over the years, it seems that I could never get enough information about that Renaissance man. My goal in life was to become a "Leonardo Da Randolph."

That goal lasted until, a little while later, I read a Classic Comic book about the life and accomplishments of Paul Robeson. The Paul Robeson story was incredible, even in comic book form. The story was even more incredible to me, not because he happened to be

Black, but because he represented the ultimate human being, a real modern day Renaissance man – a Phi Beta Kappa scholar, a superior athlete, an accomplished actor and singer. Here in one human being was the example of a strong mind, a strong body, and a strong spirit. The comic book also mentioned something about Communism, but no one could explain to me what that was, so I passed it off as okay.

Now, I had two heroes, whose lives I could use as a pattern for my own life. On the one hand, I could learn to function across a number of disciplines – art, science, and engineering. On the other hand, I could develop a strong athletic body and achieve academic excellence based on a keen intellect. Embracing these two heroes as my ultimate role models has sometimes caused trouble – I often found it difficult to fit into an ordinary, normal life. Neither Paul nor Leonardo would have tried to fit into a nine to five job, which I tried doing for many years. While I have not achieved great celebrity or even remotely reached any of the accomplishments of these great men, as role models they have served as a framework for the modest accomplishments of my life. With these role models as a backdrop, I had the openness to pursue an eclectic array of vocations and avocations ranging from acting to computer programming, to being an entrepreneur, to being an international marketing consultant -- each with equal gusto.

The summer between seventh and eighth grade, I went down to the Randolph Homestead in Marlin, Texas again. Uncle Glover and my Aunt Frankie, who had raised my Dad, were delighted to have me spend the summer. Since I was now older and stronger than I was during my previous visit, I decided that the summer was going to be about making money.

I got a job working with my cousin, Charlie Randolph, bailing hay for fifty cents per day. It was an old-fashioned hay bailer, which consisted of a mule walking around in a circle, which drove the plunger used to compress the straw into a tight bail. The plunger was withdrawn when the mule was at the outer part of the circle. As the mule walked around to the inner part of the circle, the plunger was compressed and wire could be tied around the bail that would be pushed out on the next go round. My job was to encourage the mule to keep moving around the circle. I spent most of the day going around and around in a circle. The 50 cents was all I could think about in the hot 110-degree sun as I walked behind the mule, while trying to avoid stepping in the mule's occasional deposits.

When it got too hot to bail hay, I moved on to the more lucrative job of picking cotton. The magic number was one hundred pounds per day, for which you earned $1.00. My first day in a cotton field, I picked fifty pounds. That convinced me that I had found a moneymaker. The next day, I stopped playing around with the other kids and I stopped trying to catch the little girls with their drawers down, when they went to tinkle on the edge of the cotton patch. I settled down, picked a serious hundred pounds of cotton, and earned $1.00 for that day. Now, I felt that I was in the big time. While talking to some fellow-workers, I heard about another field near the Brazos River that was paying $1.50 per hundred pounds for pulling, rather than picking, cotton. Pulling cotton goes much faster. Instead of setting your fingers to pluck the cotton out of the cotton bowl, you just grabbed the cotton bowl and cotton as one piece and put it in your sack. The ginning process was longer for pulled cotton, but the whole harvest process was much faster. I worked in this field for two days. I thought I had made my first fortune -- three whole dollars.

With my newfound expertise in pulling cotton, I was ready to branch out. By now, I was also ready to replace my ragged, hand-me-down cotton sack with a fancy new one. I found out about a truck that passed by on the highway early in the morning. If you stood by the side of the road with a cotton sack, the driver would stop and pick you up for a ride to a field a few miles north of the next town, Chilton, Texas.

I got up early the next day. Aunt Frankie put some biscuits, salmon patties, and syrup down in the bottom of an old tin syrup can, which served as my lunch pail. It was a mile walk from the house down to the highway. To my amazement, the driver stopped, and I jumped up into the truck loaded with people. About five miles up the road, the driver stopped at the general store. You could get stuff there and have it taken out of your pay at the end of the week. This was my big chance for a new cotton sack. I went into the store and found the most glorious, fancy cotton sack in captivity. It was neatly sewn canvas, with a wide shoulder strap. The length was an ideal seven feet -- not too long and not too short. Dreams were made of this stuff – my own, brand spanking new, cotton sack. I could hardly believe my good fortune. I signed for the cotton sack and jumped proudly back onto the truck.

The rest of the ride to the new cotton field was like a triumphant return to Rome. My new cotton sack and I were going to kick some serious butt today. I had never seen cotton plants that grew so high. The plants came up to my chest, but I was undaunted. I got into a rhythm and was whizzing along pulling cotton as fast as I could go. I would pay for the cotton sack today and tomorrow would be clear money. About 10 o'clock, we stopped to get a drink of water and take a brief break. Two older women at the water jug started talking about being careful when you reached for a cotton bowl. They said, "Chile, look and be sho that cotton bowl you is reaching for ain't the head of a copperhead or rattlesnake."

After that bad news, my production declined very rapidly. I spent most of the rest of the afternoon looking, rather than pulling cotton. As you might have guessed, I didn't go back the next day. I figured I had pulled enough cotton to pay for my new sack and I didn't have to go back and take the chance of tangling with any snakes. In fact, that was the end of my short-lived, cotton-picking career. I hung the sack up where everybody could admire it and I spent the rest of the summer swimming in the Brazos River with the big guys and trying to chase the little neighbor girls into the barn.

The big moment of the summer came, however, when I went to

downtown Marlin and bought myself a gray khaki shirt and matching pants at J.C. Pennys. I was now ready to go back to middle school in style. Those gray khakis were my favorite eighth grade school clothes. I wore them all the time, but I was too embarrassed to tell anyone that I had gotten them in Central Texas with money from my summer cotton picking job.

CHAPTER 10

A Naive Eighth Grader

THE SEGREGATED KANSAS City School system had a unique feature. Black kids from all over the city had to go through middle school or junior high, the eighth grade, at R.T. Coles Vocational High School. During that year, students had to decide if they would stay at R.T. Coles and pursue a trade or go to Lincoln High to prepare for college. Once a student chose, it took an act of God to change that decision (or so they would have us believe). The physical location of the schools was another big klunker. If you were in Kansas City in 1950, you would have seen that R.T. Coles (recently torn down for urban renewal) was down the hill from Lincoln. R. T. Coles was located near 18th and Tracy, a few blocks from 18th and Vine, which was one of the nerve centers of Black Kansas City. Lincoln High School was a magnificent, castle-like, red brick structure rising majestically on a hill. From just about any vantage point in the Black community, you could see Lincoln. This fact made the choice less troublesome, especially for romantic types like me. Many of us, with only the most remote chances of going to college, dreamed about going up to the castle on the hill.

Before going to R.T. Coles, I tentatively decided that I would become a brick mason like my cousin, who was earning the unheard of sum of $35 per hour. Just to be on the safe side, I was going to minor in printing technology. Typesetting was one of my eighth grade classes. That class was probably another factor that helped solidify my decision to go to Lincoln and possibly onward to college. In addition to that critical decision about my future, several major events occurred during that time in my life.

The first major event was my Dad, unknowingly, trying to sell pot (marijuana) to an undercover police officer. As part of his trucking activities, dumping stuff along the Missouri River, Dad discovered a huge crop of marijuana. Marijuana plants grew along the riverbank as far as the eye could see. During World War II, the government wanted to expand the availability of domestic hemp. So, it sponsored the planting of hemp (marijuana) along many riverbanks in Iowa, Nebraska and Missouri. Dad felt he had fallen into a gold mine. He brought enough of the stuff home to fill two foot lockers or trunks. I saw the stuff, but I had no idea what it was until the FBI and police raided our apartment in the middle of the night with drawn guns. That was a very scary experience. They handcuffed Dad and dragged him away. Of course, I was mortified when my Dad's name and our address appeared in a headlined, half column story in the Kansa City Star newspaper. It was not fun to explain to my classmates. Later, when I saw my Dad at the trial, I made an emotional outburst -- "Please don't take my Daddy away." I don't know if that did it, but he got placed on probation for 4 or 5 years rather than prison.

Another major event had to do with me getting up the nerve to call the most beautiful girl in the eighth grade -- Raedell Dean. Getting Raedell's phone number was one of my biggest eighth grade moments. Not having the nerve to ask her directly for her phone number, I found out where she lived and let my fingers do some walking through the phone book. I called, and she answered the phone. To my amazement, she was quite gracious and sweet. I made her my phone pal. Even though I had no idea how far out of her league I was, I continued to call her two or three times a week. I think I said hello to her while passing in the hallway only three or four times during our stay at R.T. Coles. However, I couldn't imagine stopping to talk to her face to face. It was enough for me to talk to this goddess on the phone occasionally.

Raedell was my major romantic focus until that fateful day in music class that changed my entire perspective on women. This indeed was another major event. It was a typical day in our eighth grade music class. Ms. Washington, the main music teacher was working with the class to get us to sing, "Joshua Fit De Battle of Jericho." I had not had much real contact with her assistant, Ms. Paige. Ms. Paige was the woman who played the school's old upright piano as Ms. Washington took us through our vocal paces. Most of that semester, we sat across the room from Ms. Paige. We (and I speak for most of the boys present at the time) loved watching the back of Ms. Paige's head and the sway of her broad hips as she tried to keep up with our wildly off-key chorus.

Until that earth-shattering day in February, Ms. Washington was the focus of my older woman crush. Ah, Ms. Washington, what a beautiful woman she was. She was on the tallish side. She was hefty, but not fat. Ms. Washington (I never knew her first name) wore her smooth black hair in a tight bun at the back of her head. Her impeccable skin glowed with a soft reddish copper tone. She evoked an image of the proud, plains Indians, from whom she surely must have descended. She was the type of woman you would call handsome.

Although I was too young to masturbate, Ms. Washington was, for a long time, the object of my pre-masturbatory fantasies. That was true until that fateful February day. That day, almost halfway through the class period, when Ms. Washington couldn't tolerate the extremely off-key boy's section any longer. I didn't know that much about music, but I suspect we were all singing in our own individual keys with our own individual tempos.

Apparently, Ms. Washington thought that having the boys cluster around the piano would help us to get at least on the same key. As we gathered around the piano, I pushed my way to the front. I wanted to get close to Ms. Paige, so I could watch her fingers glide across the keyboard. In the midst of the shuffling around and boys pushing each other, I suddenly felt as though a bolt of lightning had struck me. I saw the front of Ms. Paige for perhaps the first time. In an instant, I decided that she was a handsome fox like Ms. Washington. She, too, had beautiful, smooth black hair gathered in a bun in the back. Now, I was torn between my long-standing Ms. Washington fantasy and this new fantasy hatching in my thirteen-year-old brain. In that moment, I wanted to ravish Ms. Paige. I wanted to make her my sex slave.

Finding myself in the middle of this fantasy transition caused me to stumble with the words in the song. It was very hard to concentrate. In a brief moment, which seemed like a year, I thought I caught a whiff of Ms. Paige's perfume. My body trembled and my mind began to swirl. I was just about to spin off into another galaxy, when suddenly; my eyes locked onto them -- the two lovely mounds on Ms. Paige's chest. I had seen many lovely mounds by then, but this time, my breathe was completely taken away, with the sight of Ms. Paige's cleavage. I felt faint and my knees wobbled when I noticed the tuft of salt-n-pepper gray hairs growing between her breasts. I have never seen anything, not even a naked girl that was as sexy as that tuft of gray hairs. I wanted so desperately to reach out and touch them. I wanted to nuzzle my face in them. I wanted to lick them. Somehow, this tuft of breast hair was the sexiest thing I had ever seen, even in the contraband nudist magazines some of the guys had shown around school.

Although Ms. Paige was too discrete to notice, I must have stared directly at them for what seemed like an eternity. My mind seemed to want to leave my body and not return. I was swept up in an erotic whirlwind that gives me pause, even today. Thank God. I was too excited to get an erection.

Later that semester, another major event occurred. My acting career almost died on the vine. I took a speech class, because the idea of learning to give speeches appealed to me. One of the major class activities was memorizing and reciting poems in front of the class. One poem in particular grabbed me. It was Sir Alfred Lord Tennyson's "Crossing the Bar." It was a poem about not making a fuss after someone died. He was telling people how to be cool in the face of death. I loved that poem, and recited it with great feeling. Our teacher, Mrs.

Carter, taken with my interpretation, invited me to one of the city's graveyards to recite that poem as part of an upcoming Memorial Day Service. I agreed. On Memorial Day, I turned over in bed, and realized that I was petrified at the idea of reciting a poem in a graveyard. I hadn't mentioned this engagement to my parents and they weren't aware that I needed to get to the graveyard that morning. I rolled over, and went back to sleep.

The next day at school, Mrs. Carter did not say anything to me. Moreover, I just pretended that nothing had happened. About thirty-five years later, at a high school reunion, I took the initiative to apologize to Mrs. Carter for this folly. She was very gracious about the whole thing. Whether she remembered or not, I felt relieved to apologize finally, for leaving her in a lurch.

So, between the marijuana raid, Raedell Dean, Ms. Paige and my nearly aborted acting career, junior high school was an exciting year. I was ready for the ninth grade and the move up to the castle on the hill – Lincoln High School. That decision was driven primarily by my previous summer of hard work. I reasoned that, *"Only College could save me from that kind of life time of drudgery."* Later, I learned how right I was.

Somehow, during my eventful year in junior high school, my Dad stumbled into the landscape business. After recovering from his arrest, and second reprieve from a prison term, Dad got a temporary job using his truck to haul sod. That was his introduction to the landscaping or sod laying business. Working hard at the landscape business was a much easier way to spend his five-year probation term. Dad's discovery of the landscaping business was the first time that I was exposed to hard manual labor. The idea of that type of hard manual labor for the rest of my life was another big factor in my decision to go to Lincoln to try to go to college.

CHAPTER 11

The Castle On the Hill

THE SUMMER BETWEEN Junior High and High School was a very tough summer. For the first time, I became a full member of Dad's landscaping crew. At first, my job was a kid's job. I was responsible for watering the sod once it was laid. During the first part of the summer, I played around, skipping in and out of the water. Dad and I would get up at 4 or 5 AM to take the truck out to the country, load it with sod, and bring it back to create instant grass for new housing developments.

The sod business was relatively simple. A sod contractor went out, found a group of new houses being developed, and agreed to provide new grass for the yards. He then went out and contracted with a farmer to cut a few acres of his pastureland into rolls of sod. A sod-cutting device was used to scrape up long rows that looked like two-foot wide carpets with about two inches of dirt and grass on top. These long carpets were then marked, i.e. cut into five-foot lengths. This created a small five-foot by two-foot grass carpet.

The individual grass carpets were then rolled, by hand, for loading onto a truck for the trip to the job site. The critical success factor was to get the sod cut, marked, rolled, loaded onto the truck, laid and watered at the job site as fast as possible. Depending on the distance to the farm source, the ideal day was three loads or five-hundred square yards per day laid, and ending with a load on the truck for delivery first thing the next morning.

Toward the end of the summer, I was fourteen and had grown a few inches. This caused me to drift into the role of setting an example for the rest of the work crew. I had to work faster and harder than any member of the crew. I was no longer a kid hanging out with his Dad. I became the lead worker. Sometimes during the summer, when the "casual labor" (drunks and winos), couldn't be found to form a crew, Dad and I would go out and do most of the operation ourselves. In that case, we were lucky to get two loads of sod done for the day.

During this period, my truck-cab schooling began. Dad and I spent many hours together every day. At first, it was fun to be with my Dad, but that faded as soon as I realized that the cab of the truck was really a classroom. It was an opportunity for Dad to give me one of his non-stop lectures from his long list of subjects. The subjects varied from "How to Manipulate the White Man for Survival and Profit" to "How Many Children Was Too Many." He would get very upset when I dozed off to sleep out of boredom. However, one particular lecture that has stuck with me and has served me well was the "No Such Thing as Can't" lecture. Dad went on for about two hours on the fact that the word "can't" didn't exist. He said, "There is no justification for the use of that word." My feeble arguments notwithstanding, he made the point that, "Can't is a word that should be erased from the English language." To my surprise a day or two later, his argument struck me as making sense. I began erasing the word "can't" from my vocabulary a short time after that fateful truck-cab training session. Although it has sometimes gotten me into trouble, operating my life as if the word "can't" didn't exist has brought me some enormous personal and professional rewards.

For a number of summers, I was very convenient for Dad's business, because I was paid only with lunches or a small allowance for movies on the weekends. Occasionally, I got to drink a beer with the crew at the end of the workweek. Also, I could be cajoled into working harder than the rest of the crew, if for no other reason than pride. Never having learned to hit a baseball curve, I have often wondered if little league baseball would have been a better alternative for me as a fourteen year old.

By the end of the summer, I had become a superb lead worker. I took a day off for class pre-enrollment before school actually started. During pre-enrollment at Lincoln, I chose Latin, Algebra, and English; because during the summer I had decided that I was going to become a medical doctor.

High school was the first time that parents had to pay for books. For some unknown reason, my Dad could not come up with the money to buy my books. As a result, without text books, I had to stay out of school for about three weeks. There was no choice but to wait until I could afford books. I also needed a decent pair of shoes that were not water and mud soaked. By the time I got into the classroom, I was frightened about the possibility of failing. During that same six-week grading period, I made A's in Latin, and English and a D in Algebra. I had missed too many basics in Algebra. That was the beginning of my personal struggle with Mathematics, which I eventually won.

In 1951, we moved to a large house in a small "black-pocket" neighborhood. Kansas City had three or four of what I call "black pocket" neighborhoods. These were predominantly White neighborhoods on the edge of which Blacks might occupy several blocks of houses. These neighborhoods were generally further away from the center of the city and bound on the backside by either a major street or a large open area with trees or landfill. For example, Lincoln was on 22nd street and we lived on 57th street, a long 45-minute public bus ride. That was probably the only reason that I wasn't asked by Dad to go to the job sites after school.

I was flabbergasted to find that in high school, they actually gave us almost two hours each day to study in something called "study-hall." I used those two hours as if they were a precious gift. I would conjugate Latin nouns. I would review English sentence structure and try to understand Algebra. I was determined not to fail. I worked like a beaver during those precious study periods. Working hard in study hall meant that I didn't have to lug books home on the bus -- that was long before the era of backpacks. One day, Dad noticed I wasn't bringing books home. He got angry and insisted that I bring them back and forth from school. I tried to explain the "study-hall" concept to him, but he refused to believe me. There had been nothing in his third grade educational experience that matched that idea. So, I started bringing books home. I would wave them around so everyone could see them, throw them in a corner, and then go out to play basketball with the neighborhood guys. Dad did not have to worry about me doing the best I could in school. After all, school was my way out of a life of getting up at 4 AM and laying sod. The lesson of hard work was as important as the lessons I had learned about what "rich white folks" did or didn't do.

Lincoln High School was an interesting environment in many ways. For the first time I was exposed to middle-class Blacks. Several of the students' dads and mothers were doctors, dentists, or postal workers. Given the horrific job discrimination and the racist Kansas City environment of the 1950's, Blacks with a steady job at the Post Office were considered middle class.

Many of the guys wore tailored suits, ties, and Stacy-Adams shoes. Many of them had cars. Tailored suits or slacks were something that every kid aspired to own. Stacy-Adams shoes symbolized excellence, taste, prosperity and the ultimate of elegance at Lincoln High School and, I found out later, in the Black culture. These shoes had a smooth knob toe that could be highly polished. The knob toe surrounded by crushed, soft leather gave these shoes a distinctive style. Sometimes, these shoes were referred to as "knobs." The fashion plate dudes had two pair of Stacy-Adams -- a black pair and a brown pair. I began to dream about owning at least one pair of those incredible shoes.

It was frustrating for me to see how these middle-class Blacks dressed because all of a sudden, I was a misfit again. I wasn't a down-and-out welfare kid but I wasn't middle class either. The middle-class ideas resulting from my "rich white folks" upbringing weren't enough to make me truly middle-class. I owned only three pairs of jeans and my trusty gray khaki suit, which I soon had to abandon in the face of frequent snickers from my homeroom buddies. Being a misfit wasn't new. By now, I knew how to compensate by being smart and speaking perfect English. By the end of my first year, my name was called out loud in an all-school assembly. I was the recipient of an award for excellence in Latin. I had made mostly A's and B's in Latin during the year. Although no one else cared, it was a source of great personal pride for me.

The summer was hot in many ways. Some friends of my Dad's decided to move in with our family. I think Dad was starting to have trouble meeting the mortgage payments, so we took in roomers. Our new housemates included a 12-year-old daughter, Yvonne. We kept sniffing around each other but were both too young to date. One evening, while we were left downstairs to do the dishes, I started "accidentally" bumping up against her. This was my version of the seduction game we often played in the hallways at school. She was twice as frightened and nervous as I was. Knowing that the adults were somewhere upstairs, I enticed her to stand with me on a landing behind the door that led down to the basement. I leaned against her so she could feel my engorged penis. She started squirming, not being sure what was going on or what was going to happen. I lifted her dress and tried to get my penis into the waistband of her panties. I was thinking, *"If I can get it in her panties, I'll be able to get it into her eventually."* All of a sudden, there was a massive explosion of hot liquid all over everything. It scared the hell out of both of us. While we stood there trying to figure out what had happened, her father shouted for her to come upstairs. Poor kid! She pulled her dress down over that mass of "goo" and ran upstairs like a scared rabbit. I jumped into my bed, pulled the covers over my head and waited for the worst. However, nothing happened. During the night, the wrath of God did not descend taking me away to fire and damnation.

Her family lived with us for another three months, but Yvonne wouldn't come near me. She wouldn't stay in a room alone with me for more than ten seconds. Our previous encounter was too frightening for her. I learned that about three years later, Yvonne got pregnant. I guess I lucked out by not becoming a father at age fourteen.

The summer of 1951 was a very difficult one for Dad's sod business. It rained almost every day so we couldn't go to work. I kind of had the summer off. I hung around the house shooting songbirds with my BB gun and hoping for more "gooey" encounters. It never occurred to me that blue jays and cardinals were not fair game.

One afternoon, perhaps out of boredom, I decided that it was time to learn to smoke, after finding an old corncob pipe in the basement. I collected a bunch of Camel cigarette butts from my stepmother's ashtrays. That was before Camels had filters. I stripped out enough tobacco to fill the pipe bowl and sneaked out onto the back porch for a little smoke. A very few puffs later, I decided that I was probably going to be the first Black kid to ever turn green. That thought didn't stop me and I persevered.

I puffed away until additional rampant waves of nausea hit my stomach. About the same time that the peaks and valleys of my stomach were beginning to roll like the open sea, my stepmother called me to go to the grocery store. I must have looked and smelled awful, but she didn't say anything. She gave me a list of what to get at the store. As I stood there trying to keep from throwing up all over her, I started to think about the half-mile walk to the store. That did not help the nausea at all. I practically crawled to the store and back. I was, from that moment in my brief history, completely cured of the smoking bug. After I recovered, I was very aware of the meaning of that old cliché -- if God had intended for us to smoke he would have put a chimney in our heads. After that experience, I was ever thankful that smoking was never an option for me. I didn't even care if "rich white folks" smoked or not.

The great Kansas City flood of 1951 contributed to my Dad's ongoing series of business and financial failures. Without Dad's permission, one of his workers, who had borrowed the truck to go home, had tried to make some extra money by rescuing his friend's household goods from the flood area. He got out in time, but the truck was left to the ravages of the Missouri River floodwaters. After the floodwaters receded, I went down to that area with Dad to see the truck, an old two-ton 1946 Ford. It was barely sticking up out of a sea of silt. Somehow, shortly after this disaster, Dad was able to get another truck. But, the continuing lack of income caused us to be foreclosed and, subsequently, evicted from our house. We spent several nights sleeping in the truck until Dad somehow found an old man with whom we could share an apartment in the inner city. It was not quite the slums but it was right on the edge.

For the remainder of that summer, my days were spent helping our seventy-year-old landlord hang wallpaper at several of his former girl friends' apartments. Even though he was a bit shaky, he was meticulous about matching flower patterns and the like in the rooms we papered. I was his paste up man. I learned to mix paste, cut the paper, fold it and hand it to him as he went about papering the walls. I got paid a few bucks per project.

By the end of summer, we had moved to another Black-pocket suburb in the same area where my cousins lived. That area, called Leeds, had the reputation of being a neighborhood for poor, countrified Blacks that you wouldn't want your daughter to marry. It was the kind of neighborhood where poor people kept chickens and pigs in their back yards so they could eat regularly. Getting back to school was not quite as bad as the previous year. I had to coast only a week without books.

CHAPTER 12

Dancing to Grab the Brass Ring

THE SECOND YEAR of high school was a little easier. Homeroom was the first period every day. I had three or four solid buddies – my homeroom buddies. One day, I made a horrendous error. While filling out some papers for the start of school, I accidentally wrote my middle name, Henry, in front of my first name. When the homeroom teacher got the papers, she started asking in loud, unforgivable tones: "Who is Henry Randolph?" I almost died. My buddies started a little chorus action, "Henry Randolph, where is Henry Randolph?" They knew exactly where and who Henry Randolph was. My homeroom buddies now had a way to rib me and they often did. They had me by the short ones. Ever after that day, even thirty-five years later at high school reunions, I was known as "Henry Randolph" by this small, select group of homeroom buddies.

Somehow, they sensed how violently I hated my middle name. While growing up, my stepmother had always called me Bob Henry. That wasn't so bad until she yelled it out over the neighborhood. In addition, it usually seemed to happen just when I was about to win a marbles game. It often happened when I was about to kiss some little girl, whom we had lured into our "Boys Only" clubhouse. My stepmother always seemed to call me at very inopportune moments.

One day, in 1953, my stepmother made a startling announcement -- she was pregnant. What a surprise that was. She had gone to the doctor with a lingering cold and had come back pregnant. Dad was walking around like the Cheshire cat that ate the canary and my stepmother became the hormonally unbalanced wicked witch of the Midwest. She had a tough time being pregnant for the first time at age thirty-two; especially since she was not prepared for the pitter, patter of tiny feet. My little brother, Martin Darnell was born in April 1954.

Academically, the second year of high school was not too eventful. By now, I had dropped the idea of becoming a medical doctor. I was thinking about being an architect, because of my experiences in drafting class. Becoming an architect seemed a lot less demanding and less costly than becoming a doctor. I stuck with the architect idea until I found out that it would take a minimum of five years of college to become an architect. I reasoned that I didn't have five years to spend in college. I wanted to get out and live as fast as possible. In spite of the five years, I later learned that becoming an architect would not have been a wise choice for me.

During my second year in high school, I also decided that, in addition to being a great architect, I was going to be a great writer. That decision meant that I was not going to read books any more. This approach would insure that whatever I wrote would be original. My writing voice was going to be pure and unadulterated by any other writer's work. I scrupulously avoided courses like English Literature that required reading novels. This preposterous writing myth lasted until my first year in college. I still, however, read a lot of magazine and encyclopedia articles. My favorite pastime was to open an encyclopedia at some random page and read about the things on that page or in that section.

By this time, I had discovered girls but I felt I didn't have a lot to offer. I made a couple of fleeting passes at getting something going with Doris Woods but that effort fell flat on its face. By now, she was going out with the guy she eventually married. My aggressive pursuit in the seventh grade had gone for naught. Occasionally, in the hallway, I would see girls, like Raedell Dean, from junior high school days. But, it was painfully obvious that I didn't have a chance with

Raedell, or anyone like her, in this new environment. I had no car, no money, no cool clothes, and no claim to fame. I didn't even play football or anything.

One day, hoping to put an end to my non-status with girls, I decided to go out for the basketball team. On the afternoon of the try-outs, I suited up in my black, high top tennis shoes and my baggy white gym shorts. I ran out on the floor to get into the warm up flow for a few baskets. I heard a couple of the regulars say in overt stage whispers, "Who is this punk? Where did he come from? Who does he think he is?" Since I couldn't escape by melting into the floor, I kind of ambled over to the side of the court, shot a couple more baskets, and quietly dissolved into the showers.

It had not occurred to me that there was an unwritten rule that you didn't just "try out for the team" in order to be on the basketball team. I had no clue that all the basketball guys hung out together and were part of a clique that I clearly didn't fit into. I rather suspected this was true of the football players too. I decided not to embarrass myself again by trying out for football. I got my comeuppance in high school sports.

Martha Keys was a bright ray of sunlight in my otherwise murky existence. Martha was also my first significant rejection by a female. She had a major impact on how I viewed girls for a long time afterwards. During the second year of high school, I was going along, rather resigned to my lack of an interested girl friend. Then one day, I got a note passed to me from one of Martha's girl friends. The note said, "Hi, my name is Martha Keys. I think you are cute." Wow! I had to read the note again to make sure I wasn't dreaming. At that point, I started thinking about getting married, buying a house, and never leaving Martha's side. But, when I came to my senses, I realized that I should probably get to know her before finalizing the marriage plans. I sent a note back that I would like to walk her home from school, which she accepted.

The day finally arrived for me to walk Martha home. We met right after school. I really had to work hard at being cool and not saying something stupid. It turned out to be a pleasant time. I felt very comfortable being with her. It was also great that a lot of her friends and my friends saw us together. The rumor mill would soon acknowledge that Robert Randolph and Martha Keys were an item. I felt like a million dollars, walking around with my chest poked out a mile. We had a couple of movie dates before I summoned up the courage to kiss her. Since I didn't yet have anyone to compare her to, I thought she was a good kisser. Because her brother was a member of the El Capitans -- the school's elite boys club -- Martha and I received an invitation to their formal Spring dance.

I was in seventh heaven, in spite of the fact that I couldn't dance. We had a month, however, to get me into some kind of dancing shape. Martha was determined to help solve my problem. One school holiday, we met at her house. We spent most of the day engaged in a marathon dance lesson. In between, I would think about what might happen if her brother wasn't in the next room. However, I did manage to restrain myself.

Our session was so bad that we had to stop trying to dance together and work on whether I could muster up anything that might look like rhythm. I was beginning to think that I was the only Black kid in America that didn't have rhythm. This was my first confrontation with proving that the old stereotype is not true, Blacks don't all have rhythm. Every time I hear the instrumental version of a tune called "Night Train," I remember the hours spent in the middle of Martha's living room stomping on one foot trying to follow the beat. After that session and a couple more sessions, we gave up and decided that we would count on a miracle.

The night of the big dance came. I rented a tuxedo with all the trimmings for the occasion. I talked a buddy that had a car, into double dating. As was the custom, a group of us made reservations at the Street Hotel Restaurant near 18th and Vine for an after-dance dinner. I stopped at the florist and picked up a corsage for Martha. This was going to be the date of the century.

When I picked Martha up at her house, I noticed a bit of coolness but I thought it was merely an attempt to curb her excitement. By the time we got to the dance, I was fawning all over Martha as if she was the last woman on earth. About half way through the evening, as I was delivering another cup of punch, Martha hit me with the news. She said in a fairly cold tone: "This is going to be our last date. I won't be able to see you after tonight."

It took a while for me to comprehend what she was saying. When the full meaning of her statement hit me, I was devastated. *"What did she mean? Why? What did I do? What didn't I do?"* Finally, I found the voice to speak the questions out loud: "What do you mean? Why won't you see me again? Have I done something wrong?"

She kept repeating the same sentence over and over: "This is our last date. I can't go out with you anymore."

With my feathers completely crushed, I gave up and asked if we could still do the dinner thing, which was paid for in advance. She agreed to go. In the car, on the way to the restaurant, I tried to soften her up with some kisses. She was cordial, but still gave no explanation. After we sat down at our table, I went to play the jukebox to lighten up the atmosphere. I found a Nat King Cole song called "Answer Me My Love." I played it about ten times. As Nat Cole sang: "Answer me, oh my love. Just what sin have I been guilty of?.............." we ate our chicken dinners.

I dropped Martha at her house. I gave her a peck on the cheek and jumped back in the car to go home. I was miserable. I had my buddy let me out of the car a few blocks from my house so I could walk and think a bit before going to bed. I swore that I would never let a girl hurt me that way again. I didn't see much of Martha after that, except passing in the hallway. To this day, I don't know what caused this sudden rejection. I suspect that her mother squelched things because I was from the other side of the tracks -- a poor boy that lived in Leeds. I guess she didn't realize I had a "rich white folk's" upbringing and that where I lived had nothing to do with my character.

Occasionally, my mother would send me "California" clothes that she had been given by the rich white folks for whom she worked. These clothes were too way out for a kid in my high school, but I wore some of them anyway. I was so far out of the mainstream that I almost set my own, eclectic style. One day I went to school wearing bright red suspenders with my jeans. I got some funny looks in the hallway, but there seemed to be more of an attitude of curiosity, than outright hostility. So I tried other outlandish combinations.

Dad and I worked together a lot that summer. About mid-way through the summer, my mother sent me a train ticket to come visit her in Los Angeles. Miracle of miracles, Dad let me go. I could hardly believe it. That summer in Los Angeles was interesting and very different from my previous summers. There wasn't that much to do during the day so, I spent most of the day in Mom's living room listening to the radio and dancing from one end of the room to the other. I was determined to learn how to dance by the time I went back to school.

My Mom had remarried. Her new husband, George Watson, was an Engineer who, unfortunately, was an alcoholic. Every evening he would stop at the store and buy a quart of beer and a pint of vodka. He was a quiet, almost pleasant drunk who seemed to use the alcohol to relieve the daily stress of being the only Black Civil Engineer in the Los Angeles City Engineering Department. He was very kind to me. To give me a preview of life as an educated Black man, he took Granddad and me to dinner at the Statler-Hilton in downtown Los Angeles. I stayed at this hotel about twenty years later, while traveling on business. It didn't look as awesome as it did the night when the three of us had a first-class meal there.

Three for Dinner
Granddad, Me and George -- On our
way to a big night out at the LA Statler-Hilton

Before it was time to go back to Kansas City, Mom and Grand-dad got together and took me shopping. They wanted to make sure that I had some nice clothes to wear back to school. This worked better, because I was able to pick out clothes that at least partially fit my high school scene. I didn't dare ask for a tailored suit or a pair of Stacy Adams shoes. That couple of months in Los Angeles did more for my self-esteem than two years of therapy might have done. I came roaring back to my third year of high school more like a hip cat from California than a misfit from Lebanon. I was ready to get into the social fray.

CHAPTER 13

Popularity Without Portfolio

DURING THE BEGINNING of my third year in high school, I began coming out of my shell. In spite of the fact that I was becoming increasingly popular, I still had no steady girlfriend. With my new, finely honed dancing skills, I went to every party I could find. From the minute I arrived to the minute I left, I danced my ass off.

Occasionally, I found myself in an alley with a couple of buddies, taking a hit off a half-pint bottle of cheap bourbon. This was something I said I would never do but I finally succumbed to the call of the wild. Besides, the cheap liquor supplied a lot of dancing energy.

This was a truly hot year. The alternative boys club called the Del Magnus' inducted me into their group. Our club sweaters, which we wore once a week, were royal blue. We were the misfits, and the lower-class boy's club. We were also social climbers. The El Capitans were the "other" boy's club sanctioned by the school. Their sweaters were maroon. The El Capitans got all the jocks, middle class dudes and the cool chicks. Every spring they gave a traditional, formal party. The El Capitans were considered the movers and shakers -- the elite quasi-fraternity guys.

By contrast, my club, the Del Magnus', distinguished ourselves by being uncool. We drank a lot and threw a lot of parties. Those of our members that got any women, usually got the left over women, but we didn't care. We weren't overly rowdy, but we had a hell of a lot of fun. My homeroom buddies and I were the ringleaders of the Del Magnus club. We reveled in our misfit-ness. Our view of the world was that it was cool to be uncool. Although we were heavy into alcohol, we didn't smoke pot or do any kind of hard drugs. I guess we were too scared, too uncool or too unhip to do any other drugs except alcohol.

I was taking second year French and every spring the class put on a special all-school assembly with a French theme. For some strange reason, I decided to do a spot as Nat King Cole singing "Darling J'Vous Aime Beaucoup." I was determined not to take the easy way out and lip sync the song. Somehow, I was not only going to learn to sing, but I was determined to imitate Nat Cole to the extent that no one could hear a noticeable difference between us. This was an example of one of my key character flaws -- the ability to vision far beyond any current reality. It never occurred to me that I couldn't learn to sing like Nat Cole in a few weeks.

The rehearsals were awful. Poor Ms. Pendleton, the French teacher, lost about five years off her life trying to work with me to pull the thing together. It seemed that every time I stood up in rehearsal to give some glimmer of what I was going to do and how I was going to sound, my voice would crack. Those times when my voice was okay, I would forget the words. Not having a phonograph at home to play records, I borrowed one and listened to the Nat Cole record about a thousand times. Finally, I got together with a classmate named John Myles.

John was a musical genius who played several instruments and was very accomplished on the piano. Ms. Pendleton felt a lot better knowing that John would accompany me. She knew he could save the show by moving into a Chopin Concerto, with me mouthing some words, if it came to that.

We hadn't discussed wardrobe so I did what was obvious to me. To be ready for a random invite to an El Capitans' Spring formal, I had bought a cheap, white dinner jacket. I wore it with dark pants and some highly polished black shoes just as I imagined Nat Cole would do. It took almost a whole can of greasy kid stuff to slick down my hair. When it was my turn to perform, I just assumed I was Nat Cole and strolled nonchalantly about fifty feet to the microphone, in the center of the stage. It was shocking to see the reaction of the student body. Instead of the hushed silence I had expected, with every ear straining to see how closely my voice matched that of Nat Cole's, there was wild pandemonium. John started to play before the roar died down. We were half way through the song before anyone bothered to listen. John and I were a hit. I think someone had to revive Ms Pendleton backstage. Later, I took this act on the road to other high schools when we were doing exchange programs with White high schools that were in the process of desegregating.

Nat King Cole at Lincoln
Me -- Imitating Nat King Cole, singing
"Darling J' Vous Aime Beaucoup"

That was the beginning of my high school drama career. I felt that maybe I had finally discovered a way to get girls. Later that year, the drama teacher, Mr. Vaughan, invited me to audition for the annual Junior play. I was extremely flattered since I wasn't in the drama class or the drama club. The play was a typical farce that high schools often present. It called for a blustery, fatherly type. Since I was beginning to develop a big, deep voice, the role was a natural for me. I tied with one of my homeroom buddies, Bobby Jones, for the lead part. This set a precedent. I played the lead one night and he played the lead the next night. My drama career was off to the races.

Bobby and I were both thrilled to get the part. We had a lot of fun with that play. I also got a small role in the annual Senior play that year.

It was about this time that I learned that my stepmother was pregnant again. Being pregnant for a second time turned her into such a snarling beast, that Dad sent her to Dallas to live with her relatives until the baby came. That was great for me. I did the housework, helped my Dad with the cooking, and ironed my own shirts. She could never get the collars right anyway.

It suddenly dawned on me one day that I was one of the most popular boys in the Junior class but I still had no steady girl friend. This was a very frustrating situation for me. Kids were holding hands to and from school, sneaking kisses in the hallway and, according to the scuttlebutt, screwing their brains out in the back seats of cars every night, while I was worrying about how soon I would need glasses. That was about the time that Beverly Johnson entered stage left.

Beverly lived in my neighborhood. She was one of the people who had stayed at R. T. Coles. Rumor had it that Bev spent more time in the back seats of cars than in class. She was about 5'2" tall. She was 17, and had dark skin that seemed powdery on the surface. She didn't fit anybody's picture of a cool chick, but there was a kind of sweetness about her. Bev probably originated the concept of "Big is Beautiful." Somehow, she knew how to use her size as a part of her sensuality. Because of her reputation, I didn't want to be seen with her, but that didn't stop me from wanting to be one of her backseat lovers.

One day I saw her walking to the store near my house. Although I was very nervous about being seen, speaking to her, my hormones took over and I cranked up the courage to start a casual conversation with her about the weather. While we were talking, I slipped a very casual: "Would you go to the movies with me?" into the conversation.

To my surprise, she said, "Yes!"

"Oh my God, what have I done? What if some one sees me with Beverly? I don't even have a back seat or a car to put her in." I thought to myself. My surging hormones came to the rescue in about three tenths of a second. The hormones said, *"Take her to the movies during the week. No one will see you, not your homeroom buddies or her current boy friend or anybody. You can pretend that the date never happened."* So, I followed the advice from my hormones.

"Why don't we go to the movie next Wednesday?" I asked as casually as I could.

"That would be great. You gonna pick me up?" She asked.

"Yeah, is six okay?"

"Okay. You know where I live don't you?"

"Oh yeah, down past the pool hall?"

"Yeah that's right. I'll see you then." She answered as she walked away.

It is wonderful how Providence takes care of fools. On Wednesday evening as agreed, I picked Bev up at her door. We caught a bus that took us to a movie theater, near 18th and Vine. The theater was coincidentally called the Lincoln Theater.

I paid our way, while looking over my shoulder hoping to not see any of my homeroom buddies. As soon as we got inside, Bev nudged me to take the stairs to the balcony. Gosh, I had been to this theater lots of times, and didn't even know there was a balcony. When we got upstairs, we looked around. We were the only ones in the balcony. She pulled me along to a seat right in the middle of a sea of empty seats. As we sat down, Bev grabbed my hand and thrust it under her skirt. She wriggled and squirmed a lot until my innocent fingers were touching bare, wet flesh. This sensation of fondling a warm, wet vagina took my breath away. Just as I was about to catch my breath, she leaned over and thrust her tongue half way down my throat. At least that was the way it seemed. Out of the corner of my eye, I could see that the previews were still running. It was going to be a very long double feature.

This was the first time I had ever spent four hours with my legs crossed, with a bulging erection, with my hand in a girl's vagina and our tongues entwined. Life wouldn't ever be the same again. About three-quarters of the way through this pleasant ordeal, I had to go to the toilet. As I got up, I noticed a severe cramping kind of pain in my groin. I thought that was strange, but I felt it would go away when I peed. Peeing only made the pain more intense. By the time I got back to my seat, I was beginning to think about appendicitis. I gritted my teeth through the rest of the movie. By now, a big neon sign was flashing in my mind -- appendicitis, appendicitis, APPENDICITIS, AP-PENDICITIS!!

When we got out onto the street, I was totally perplexed and Bev was wearing a rather pleased-with-herself grin. My mind was racing a mile-a-minute. If we took the bus in one direction, we would get home. If we took the bus in the opposite direction, I could pop into the city hospital to take care of my appendicitis. Alternatively, I could put Bev on the bus for home and I could take the bus to the hospital by myself. But that wouldn't be the gentlemanly thing to do. According to a book I had read on dating and manners, it was my obligation to take her back to her doorstep. The "rich white folks" thing had me firmly in its grip. I finally decided to take Bev home and then jump back on the bus for the city hospital. Maybe I would get there before my appendix burst. So, we started the hour-long bus ride home.

By the time we got to Bev's house, I could walk upright again. I felt brave enough to walk home since I was feeling much better. I thought it was probably a good idea to wait until the next morning before dealing with my apparent appendicitis. Miraculously, it was completely gone the next day. It wasn't until three or four years later that I found out what this apparent "appendicitis" really was. Talking to one of my friends, verified that long-term arousal without release was the real cause of that painful condition called "blue balls." The next time this occurred, I knew how to deal with it.

Most of my lovers since Bev have expressed their appreciation for the training that Bev gave me, especially the kissing apprenticeship. She also taught me a lot about appreciating the fact that sexuality could come in different sizes, shapes, and colors of women.

My relationship with Bev lasted, on and off, for about two years. In the 50's this was the best of all possible worlds, having a "bad" girl to have fun with and the possibility of a "good" girl to take on dates. Bev and I were both victims of the times.

The summer was a typical hard working affair. I decided that serious partying on the weekends was a good way of making up for the daily grind of hard, manual labor. By now, I had discovered Malt liquor. The popular brand was called Country Club. It came in small, so-called pony cans. The Missouri liquor laws mandated that you had to buy beer products in threes -- three bottles of beer, three cans of beer, or three pony cans of Malt Liquor. There were two liquor stores down in the inner city that sold booze to minors with no questions asked. On the weekends, I would go to one of those liquor stores and get three pony cans of Malt liquor. Then I would walk along the dark side streets guzzling down the Malt liquor. By the time I had walked to the place where public dances were held for teenagers, I was feeling no pain. I was ready to dance my ass off. That was my regular weekend routine most of that summer.

Toward the end of the summer, it came time to retrieve my stepmother, Vida, and my new baby brother, Edward, who had been born in Dallas. Dad and I drove down to Dallas in the truck. We spent a couple of weeks there before it was time to head back to Kansas City. We put Vida, my new little brother, Edward, and my other little brother, Martin, on the train. Dad and I drove the truck down further into

Texas and stopped in a little town called Sweetwater. Dad thought it would be a good idea to take a load of watermelons back to Kansas City to pay for the trip. His plan was to sell the watermelons to a store as soon as we got back. On our way back, we blew out a rear tire just after we pulled into Muskogee, Oklahoma. I got a little nervous about the billboard sign we had seen as we crossed the town limits. This sign said: "Nigger, Don't Let Sundown Catch You in This Town." In spite of the sign, Dad was pretty cool about taking the time to get the tire fixed. I kept thinking about what we were going to do with those damned watermelons when the trouble started and how the hell, we were going to defend ourselves. Fortunately, we got the flat fixed and got out of that asshole town before sundown. This was just another expression of joy to add to all the rest of the joys of growing up black in America.

When we finally made it back to Kansas City, Dad started making the rounds of fruit stands and grocery stores trying to sell the load of watermelons. It was late August, early September and nobody wanted to pay much for watermelons, whether they were imported by hand from Sweetwater, Texas or not. Finally, we had to sell them retail. This meant off the back of the truck, up and down the streets of the Black neighborhoods. For a moment, the specter of selling watermelons off the back end of a beat up old truck in my school friends' neighborhoods struck me, but I quickly pushed that horrible thought away. Later, I had the actual, full experience of the horrendous scenario just as I had imagined. No one could guess the mortification and horrific embarrassment of seeing my homeroom buddies laughing and pointing. I could not believe that my Dad and I were slowly rolling through the streets shouting: "Watermelons!! Get your red, ripe watermelons here!! Watermelons!! Waaatermeelllooonn Man!!" It took the first three months of the school year to live that one down. Kids would sidle up to me in class or in the cafeteria and softly whisper: "Waaatermeelllooonn Man." It was a long, long three months.

CHAPTER **14**

A Very Naive Senior

I WAS IN my glory. I had it made. It was 1955 and it looked as if I would actually graduate from high school, a feat that few in my family had accomplished. I was now a big time High School Senior. I could coast on from here.

Every spring, because Lincoln High School was one of the Black academic beacons of the Midwest, colleges from all over the country came to recruit students. Juniors and Seniors were allowed to sit down with these recruiters and talk about what it was like on their ivy-cloistered campuses. Every now and then, a representative would show up from Yale or Princeton. We were a much sought after bunch.

One morning, shortly after school started, Ms. Ann Johnson, the Guidance Counselor, called me down to her office. Although I didn't know it at the time, that wonderful woman handed me my entire future in one brief meeting.

"Good morning Robert." Ms. Johnson said. "Have a seat."

I wanted to stand because I didn't expect to be in her office that long. "Thank you." I said, as I sat down, trying to mask my nervousness.

"I have been checking your grades, Robert."

"Yes Mam." I said, shifting to a bit of southern charm to soften the bad news that was coming.

"Are you planning to go to college next year?"

"Oh, yes Mam, I am." I answered.

"I think that would be a good idea. Based on your grades so far, I think you could make 'A's' and 'B's' in college."

It took a moment for me to recover. That was the most assurance I had gotten about going to college. "Thank you Mam." I said with a hint of false modesty.

"Where do you plan to go to college?"

"Oh, I was thinking about going to Yale, or Harvard." I said with all the naiveté of a seventeen-year-old kid. The limited thought I had given to this subject pointed to these two schools as the only ones worthy of my consideration. After all, I had seen their catalogs in the library and talked to a couple of admissions people. These Ivy League colleges seemed to be my kind of schools. My character flaw of "vision-versus-reality" was in full play at this point in our conversation.

Ms. Johnson was brilliant and candid in her pursuit of the subject. With scalpel-like precision, she asked pointedly, "Do your parents have any money?"

"No, they don't." I admitted sheepishly.

"How do you plan to pay for those high-priced schools?" She asked gently.

"Oh, I'll get a job and work part time." I said with all the romantic idealism I could muster. Inside I thought, *"I have no clue about what tuition actually costs, but 'where there is a will, there is a way."* As I was thinking this romantic BS, she brought me back to earth by saying.

"Robert, I'm afraid that doesn't sound very realistic. Do you have any other alternatives in mind?"

"No. I hadn't thought of any other school, but there is always Princeton." I said weakly, as it began to dawn on me that I had no money and no real plan. In retrospect, I can only marvel at the masterful way Ms. Johnson brought me to a state of reality about my college plans. Although I didn't know it at the time, this was probably the first adult conversation that I had ever had.

"Have you ever heard of the University of Kansas City?"

"No Mam, where is that?" I said with pained annoyance. Although I was too polite to say it aloud, but I was thinking: *"You got to be kidding lady." Everybody is going away to school. How could you dare even mention a hometown school to me? I would be laughed right out of my homeroom. Nobody goes to school in their own city. How absurd!"*

"It is out on Fifty-First and Troost." She said.

"You mean go to college here in Kansas City?" I asked incredulously, not wanting to show my unbridled disgust at such a terrible idea.

"Yes, it is a fine school and they are interested in having more Negro students."

"I'm not sure I want to do that. All my friends are going away to college."

"Would you consider KCU, since you don't have any viable alternatives? You may even be able to get a scholarship." She said, putting aside my childish responses.

Inside my head, I scoffed at the idea of a scholarship. I was so naïve that I thought scholarships were only for gifted students and there was no way that I could qualify.

"Well I guess KCU would be okay." I said, trying to hide my disappointment.

"There is a scholarship test session two weeks from now on a Saturday morning. Should I sign you up for that?" She asked with a commanding tone.

"Well, I guess I could take the test."

"Just do it." She cajoled. "You never know what will happen and that could be your back-up plan in case your other plans don't work out."

"But I still want to go to Harvard." I said, somewhat defiantly.

"That's great. At least you'll have KCU as an alternative and you may even receive a scholarship. I'll give you all the details about the scholarship test next week."

"Okay. Thank you Ms. Johnson." I said as I left her office.

I went back to my class feeling as if I had sidestepped the guidance counselor rather nicely and I had to keep this conversation a secret. No one, especially my homeroom buddies, could know that I was even thinking about going to college in Kansas City.

Reluctantly, I decided to take the KCU scholarship test just for fun, but I had my eyes set on bigger fish.

Seniors partied a lot that year. My homeroom buddies and I developed a regular routine. We would go to a selected liquor store and get a half pint of Four Roses or Early Times bourbon -- the really cheap stuff. We would meet in an alley or behind the stands of the football stadium. Then we would split the half-pint between four or five of us and then saunter into the football or the basketball game. Lincoln had great teams that year but we saw very little of the real action. It was pretty much of a haze.

One evening, I think it was a Friday, the guys had me go to the liquor store. I was to pick up the half-pint and meet them on a specified corner in a residential area at about 7:30. It was getting dark, but I hung around for about an hour, and nobody showed. I began to panic. I couldn't go home with this half-pint of whiskey and I absolutely couldn't throw it away. Being resourceful and at the same time, grossly underestimating reality, I decided that I would drink the half-pint. I would walk to a nearby pool hall, and hang out for a while before going home. So with this plan in mind, I started walking along dark side streets, taking big gulps from the half-pint whiskey bottle. It is a miracle I didn't get arrested. The pool hall was down in a basement and, by the time I got there, I was taking giant steps into the air. I stumbled to a chair and plopped down to watch some pool games. Soon I was seeing double and triple balls on the pool tables. I passed out for a little while. Just about the time the manager was going to ask me to leave, my long lost buddies showed up. By now, I was too drunk to be pissed-off at them.

They got me to my feet and half walked me outside. They didn't know what the hell to do with me. One of them decided that a long walk and black coffee would straighten me out. We walked for about thirty blocks. Luckily, we found an open cafe that had coffee. They started pouring black coffee into me. As soon as I would get a cup all the way down, I would excuse myself and go throw it up. That went on for a couple of hours. Finally, about 2 AM, a friend drove by in a car. We piled into the car and they drove me all the way to my house in Leeds, about 10 or 15 miles away. When we got to my house, they gently propped me up on my porch and raced off.

I'm not sure how I managed it, but I got past my parents bedroom. As I dropped into my bed like a ton of bricks, I thought *"Boy! I got it made."* Then I closed my eyes to stop the bed from spinning. It didn't stop with my eyes closed; this was really bad news. I had never been this drunk. I lay there for a while trying to think of something to do. Then I remembered a tomato that was in the back of the fridge. I had heard that tomato juice was good for hangovers. *"Surely,"* I thought, *"a whole tomato taken prior to the onset of a hangover would have some effect."* It did and very soon. I barely made it to the bathroom before tomatoey stuff started to spray all over the bathroom. But, miracle of miracles, when I got back in bed, it stopped spinning. My head stopped spinning and I was cured, at least for the moment.

About seven the next morning, I awoke to the smell and sound of bacon frying. The hangover had not yet hit in full force. I peeked out of my room and saw Dad sitting at the dinner table in a fully collected, poised manner. It was obvious that he was waiting to pounce. Well, I reasoned foolishly, that *"this won't take long; he's got to go to work."* Little did I know?

My stepmother had an awful habit of scrambling eggs right in the same pan where she had fried the bacon. So, you ended up with a cruddy-looking, nondescript, mass of yellowish egg with awful looking swirls of gritty brown fried bacon remnants. With a great triumphant flare and a "now-you-are-going-to-get-it smirk," she plunked this disgusting plate of stuff down right under my nose. By now, my hangover was welling up and Dad was winding up for one of his marathon lectures. It became clearer and clearer that this was going to be a lecture of filibuster proportions.

He started with some simple questions about when and how I got home before he launched into his full dissertation. Surprisingly, his monotone lecture, which reverberated through my aching brain like a large ping-pong ball, was not about alcohol, fire, and damnation. The main theme was his disappointment at my being out in the streets drinking. He reiterated many times his preference that I only drink at home. He reminded me of all the times he had brought beer home and encouraged me to drink it with him. He threw in all the Christmases when I had my own portion of Morgan David wine and had been occasionally allowed to have shots of whiskey just like the grownups. He only tangentially touched on the tomato-speckled bathroom, which I had to clean up later. I tried, for all I was worth, not to let my throbbing head fall into the plate in front of me. The lecture, my topsy-turvy stomach and my traumatized brain all combined to make me a basket case for the rest of the day. I never went home drunk like that again.

My popularity continued to grow but still, girls were not falling at my feet. I was dressing better. By now, I had a tailored pair of slacks and a pair of Stacy-Adams shoes. At least one day a week, I could dress like the in-crowd. Confident in my popularity, I even dared to set a style by wearing bright red suspenders again with Levi jeans. People took notice but didn't ridicule my taste. This was an amazing transformation. I had crossed over from being a misfit to being an eccentric.

While my desperate search for a "good" girl connection failed miserably, Beverly was a wonderful back up. Often when I saw her going to the store, I would talk her into coming back around dusk. We would sneak down into a basement staircase near the elementary school where I worked as a part-time janitor. I would finger her to a climax or I would squeeze my penis inside her panties and climax near her vagina. It wasn't exactly intercourse, but it was the next best thing. I was very lucky that she didn't get pregnant.

My drama career expanded. I got a role in both the Junior and Senior Plays that year. My idea and script proposal for the last farewell Senior Day all-school assembly was accepted and I got the job of producing the entire three-hour show. The only house parties I missed were during the two weeks I was at home with the mumps. I even got an invitation to the El Capitan's spring formal. In spite of all this activity, I found the time one Spring Saturday morning to go to the University of Kansas City campus and take the scholarship exam.

Almost without notice, the Senior Prom came around. I wanted desperately to go to the prom. I had my white dinner jacket from my Nat King Cole act and the only other thing I needed was a date. This became a major challenge. After a series of phone calls and hours of conversation to lead up to the question -- "Will you go to the Prom with me?" I came up empty handed. Finally, about two days before the big event, I managed to get Phyllis Mack's phone number. Phyllis was a Junior, but I was desperate. She was so sweet. After only thirty minutes of conversation, she said she would go to the Prom with me. I felt like I had won the lottery.

Senior Prom Night
Me – and my date Phyllis Mack at the Senior Prom.

Phyllis and I had a wonderful time at the Prom. I am not exactly sure why, but, for some reason, we never went out again. This was our first and last date. I guess some things are just not meant to be.

The high point of my struggles to get my Dad to understand what was going on in my life came rather unexpectedly. One evening, Mr. Vaughan, our drama teacher called to say that he would like to meet with my Dad. Dad agreed to meet with Mr. Vaughan at our house.

For months, Dad had been on my case about staying late after school. I tried to explain my involvement in school drama activities, but he only saw this activity as a distraction from my schoolwork. Mr. Vaughan came to our house about a month before graduation.

"Hello Mr. Randolph, I am Mr. Vaughan, the Drama teacher at Lincoln High School."

"Hello Mr. Vaughan. Have a seat. I hope my son hasn't messed up." Dad said.

"Oh no! Mr. Randolph, quite the contrary, he has done very well." Mr. Vaughan said.

"He has been wasting a lot of time and staying late after school. And he thought I didn't notice." Dad said with an accusing tone.

"That's true because we have been doing rehearsals for plays."

"Is that right?" Dad said inquisitively.

"As a matter of fact, Mr. Randolph, your son is very talented. On stage, he is one of the most poised students in the school." Mr. Vaughan, said.

"That is interesting. I had no idea what was going on." Dad said.

"That brings me to the purpose of my visit this evening. I came here to inform you and your son that the Black Drama Club of Kansas City has awarded your son a $100 scholarship to college in the fall."

I could hardly believe the look on Dad's face. I don't think I had ever seen him so shocked or surprised. While I was equally shocked and surprised, I recovered enough to thank Mr. Vaughan and to think to myself, *"Gotcha, Dad, gotcha good!"*

My high school days were winding down rapidly. Suddenly, Senior Day arrived. This was to be our last day at Lincoln High School.

As FDR said, "It was a day that will live in infamy." I got to school early, anticipating wrapping up the last minute details of the afternoon extravaganza that I had written and was producing. A couple of seniors offered me bourbon from their lockers, but I turned them down. One of my homeroom buddies had a gallon of wine in his locker. Somehow, I managed to stay aloof from the drunken frenzy that was developing. There was a rumor rapidly spreading throughout the school that one girl had decided to go out with a bang. Apparently, she had spread-eagled herself in the back seat of a car in the parking lot and was taking on all comers. Although I didn't get out to the parking lot, I was told that there was a line on one side of the car going in and there was a line going out. Some guys, I was told, went back for seconds. This incident shows how truly bizarre this Senior Day became.

By noon, the Vice-Principal had thrown one of my homeroom buddies, along with my old fourth grade friend Alvin Kelly, into the showers. Some seniors were passing out in their classes. I kept pushing along getting the show ready. It was a little tricky, because half the talent was drunk or sobering up. At 2:30 PM as scheduled, the curtains opened and the show was on. Since I had written and produced the show, I had a significant role. It was a thinly veiled talent show. Rather than the usual "Now, here is Joe Smith to play the Star Spangled Banner on the bass kazoo," I set a scenario in which two characters in the year 1984, picking through a rock pile, find an artifact from that ancient Senior Day, May 20th, 1955. The archeologists start to reminisce about who appeared on the show. Then the person would do their performance stage left. In between acts, I scurried around backstage to make sure the next act was not too drunk to perform.

The actual graduation ceremonies were held on June 9th downtown in Kansas City's Municipal Auditorium. Although I was far from an academic superstar, I had the honor of reciting a speech about the great, Black Haitian liberator, Toussaint L'ouverture. It made me extremely proud when I later found out that this same speech had been recited by Paul Robeson at his high school graduation. That night, during the ceremonies, I was shocked and pleasantly surprised to learn that I had received a full scholarship to the University of Kansas City, in addition to the drama scholarship that I received from Mr. Vaughan.

Let the party begin!

CHAPTER 15

Being Black Has Its Privileges

ON JUNE 10, 1955, the morning after graduation, I woke up in a strange mood. I felt the special exhilaration of knowing that I had overcome some significant hurdles so far in my life. But there was also a hint of profound sadness about leaving the tightly woven co-coon in which I had lived the previous four years. Even though I was college-bound, I started to question the need for more school. Didn't I already know most of what a person needs to know -- reading, writing, and arithmetic? At this point, I had already achieved much more than my father, who had only finished the third grade. What was left to do? I wallowed around in this inquiry of "college versus no college" for about two days. Then it was time to go back to the sod fields. After a couple of weeks of hard, gut wrenching, dirty manual labor, I regained my college aspirations. It was never a question again. I worked with Dad most of that summer. In early August, Dad, my stepmother, and my two little brothers took off in the truck to Dallas for about three weeks. They left me at home alone.

Being at home alone was going to be a real adventure. My first phone call was to Bev. I explained the situation and asked her to spend some time with me, maybe even stay overnight. She said she would come over. Then I feverishly prepared for a private party with Bev. I made a list -- booze, soda, condoms and sexy after-shave. I got on the bus, went to the liquor store, and bought a half-pint of Old

Granddad, the high priced stuff. I walked a few blocks to a drug store on the corner of 27th and Prospect, to pick up the other accoutrements.

Buying the condoms was just like a scene from the movies. This was well before the era of self-serve condoms in drug stores. In those days, you had to ask the Pharmacist behind the counter for them. As soon as I walked into the drug store, the male clerk at the pharmacy counter went somewhere, leaving a woman in his place. *"Oh my God!"* I thought. *"How am I going to ask her for rubbers?"* I fiddled around the store for a while, waiting for the male pharmacy clerk to reappear. He never did. Finally, out of sheer desperation and after practicing saying "prophylactics" a hundred times, so I wouldn't accidentally ask for "rubbers," I approached the pharmacy counter. In as deep a voice as I could muster, I said, "I would like some prophylactics, please."

"What?" She said. Horror of horrors, I had to repeat that whole sentence again.

"I would like some prophylactics, please." I blurted out nervously.

"How many do you want?" she asked, after getting my question.

I didn't know how the damned things were packaged. So, I sheepishly said, "Three, please."

She placed them down on the counter. Trying desperately, not to make eye contact, I picked up the small package of condoms as nonchalantly as possible. I paid for them and practically ran out of the store. I was never happier to get out of a store in my life.

I called Bev as soon as I got home to make sure she was still coming to my house the next day. She showed up about thirty minutes late. I was beginning to get scared that she wouldn't show up. Trying to be "Mister casual," I attempted to make some small talk. Inside my head, my mind was shouting: *"Get her in the bedroom quick!!"* Sensing that she had all the power in this situation, Bev became a tease, stalling and taking her time before getting down to action.

"Would you like a drink?" I asked.

"What you got?"

"I got some Old Grandad bourbon. Is that okay?"

"Oom. I like that stuff." She said.

I jumped right up from the couch and gave her a big glass of whiskey. Then I continued with my not so subtle: "get-your-pants-off-fast" repartee.

Finally, I took her by the hand and led her into my bedroom. I kissed her and positioned her so that she fell back on the bed with me on top of her. Fumbling under her skirt with one hand, I got the condoms out. Then I started putting one on. In my excitement, I only got it half on, before I plunged between her outstretched legs. I was doing okay until the thought of getting her pregnant seared its way through my other brain. My enthusiasm wilted like a week-old flower out of water. Hoping booze would rekindle my passion, I ran into the other room to get some liquid courage. When that didn't work, I thought a change of venue might help.

Dragging Bev by the hand, I took her into my parent's bedroom. With Bev spread-eagled on the edge of my parent's bed, I started fiddling with the second condom. It broke. I tore off the broken piece and entered her again. I stopped just at the critical moment, when I felt the condom slipping off inside her. I fished the rubber out and decided to take a rest. Later, I broke the third condom while trying to put it on. That was the last straw. I gave up in utter frustration. We sat and talked for a while and then I sent Bev home. I was too frustrated to walk her home. That was the last time I went out with her. The entire month of September was hell. I was scared to death that Bev might have gotten pregnant. I kept a very low profile during that time. This was a valuable lesson; never again would I buy only a three-pack of condoms.

While I was sweating bullets about Bev, the time came to go to college. Every morning I had to walk about a mile to catch the streetcar to school. The first day on campus was almost as traumatic as my first day of school back in Lebanon. The difference this time was the sea of white faces. My "rich white folks" training was going to come in handy. It wasn't such a big deal after all. I had learned to speak like "rich white folks." I had the manners of "rich white folks." Finally here I was, at a school with "rich white folks." I had come full circle. It turned out that my first impressions were false. There were also many poor white folks at Kansas City University (KCU).

In 1955, KCU was a small, private school, with a strong emphasis on academics and Liberal Arts. The original intent of the school's founders had been to create another University of Chicago with even greater academic freedom. The Dental and the Pharmacy Schools were the best in the Midwest.

Basil North, someone I had known only casually in high school, popped up out of nowhere. I had no idea that he was going to KCU. He became my new, instant "homeroom" buddy. I was shocked to learn that the guidance counselor, Ann Johnson, had also talked him into a scholarship at KCU.

In high school, Basil had been a "big man on campus." He had even managed to get himself elected to President of the graduating class of 1955. He always dressed impeccably in tailored suits and Stacy-Adams shoes. He was a real cool dude. He knew how to talk to girls. He not only knew how to talk to them but he knew how to get beyond responses such as, "Nice girls don't do that!" Basil was middle class by virtue of the fact that his father worked at the Post Office. Oddly enough, his father was related to some of the people who lived in Lebanon. It was truly a small world. While there were considerable differences between Basil and me, we had the common goal of doing well academically so we could continue to go to school. We built a strong friendship that has lasted more than fifty years.

Shortly, after arriving at KCU, I learned about the true nature of the Victor Wilson scholarship I had received. This scholarship was available to any student who had lived in Kansas City for 10 years (I had stretched that requirement a bit). The scholarship was renewable year-to-year through graduate school as long as the student maintained at least a "B" average. The terms of the scholarship were a serious incentive to do well academically.

About 30% of the students at KCU had received this scholarship. I also later learned that this same scholarship was available to go to Yale. For me the possibility of going to Yale was a closed case.

Including Basil and me, there were about fifteen Blacks out of a student body of 2,400 on the KCU campus. Five of us were from my senior class at Lincoln High School. We became a close-knit group. While we did make other friends around the campus, we tended to hang out together in the student union when there was time. Occasionally, we would start a large bid whist card game with partners coming and going between classes. Since I split most of my time between classes, the library and traveling for two hours a day on the streetcar, I had only the slightest semblance of a social life. It consisted mostly of an occasional game of bid whist or talking to one of the Black student nurses who visited the campus for the academic part of their training. I particularly liked one student nurse from Oklahoma, but since I had no money or car, I didn't dare ask her for a date. I felt that I had to be content with our occasional conversations in the student union.

John Green was a mysterious member of the Blacks-on-campus group. When he showed up, none of us had any idea about who he was. John seemed friendly enough. He was a bit older, more reserved and serious than the rest of us. Subsequently, we learned that John had dropped out of Lincoln High School and joined the Air Force in 1948. He was just returning from a second four-year hitch in the Air Force with his last tour spent in London, England. While Basil and I must have seemed like a couple of teenyboppers to him, he was always cordial and gracious to us. Perhaps that is why, many years later, John became my very best friend.

While John was a very mysterious character, the one thing we learned about him, was that he was an incredible writer. Basil, who was in John's freshman English Composition class, spread the word. The English teacher had read from one of John's compositions as an example of fine writing. Basil and I were jealous, but we felt proud that a brother could set a standard like that.

When I got to college, I had no idea about a major course of study; all I knew was that I wanted a job. My Dad came up with the outlandish idea that I should major in Chemistry, discover an important compound like Nylon and retire at age 30 as a millionaire. This sounded like a good plan to me, so I started naively down that path. The first semester, I took Chemistry 101. I also took another stab at math by taking a course in College Algebra. This was my last chance to resolve my long-standing ambivalence towards math. I took French Reading and English Composition. If I had had better advice from my Student Adviser, I would have taken a less ambitious course load to ensure the renewal of my scholarship. And, here again, I was left to operate out of my overblown ability to underestimate current reality and to not play it safe.

Basil made the Dean's list for academic achievement, assuring his scholarship renewal, while I made only a "C" plus average, losing my scholarship renewal chances. It was a scary, frustrating time for me. The daily commute became a horrendous burden. Somehow, I managed to beat off my Dad's demands to work with him every afternoon. He couldn't imagine why I needed to do "all of that studying." After all, he had been tops in his third grade class without studying a lot. Obviously, this meant that, according to him, "I wasn't too smart."

Toward the end of the first semester, my campus buddies from Lincoln and I were all shocked and deeply saddened when we heard through the grapevine about the untimely death of one of our most beautiful classmates, Raedell Dean. She apparently died from a botched abortion. It was especially painful for me to lose what had been my beautiful, sweet, phone pal – the first girl I ever talked with on the phone in the eighth grade. She was only eighteen. It was very difficult for me to understand how someone so young and so beautiful could die.

The second semester wasn't much better than the first semester. I earned about the same grades. The one bright spot was an "A" I made in College Algebra. In fact, I was exempted from having to take the final exam because I did so well on tests during the semester. Given my previous struggles with Algebra, this result was exhilarating. Suddenly, all of my high school Algebra work came together. It all made perfect sense. Finding out at age eighteen that you are not mentally retarded is a truly rewarding experience.

My weak overall grade point average and the prospect of losing my scholarship for the next year, left me depressed and devastated. I figured there must be some way for me to get the money to enroll next year. Tuition, by the way, was only $260 per semester. Working for Dad during the summer, I made sure I was paid. I managed to save enough for books and tuition for the first semester.

CHAPTER **16**

Surviving the Circumstances

IN THE FALL of 1956, KCU opened its first dormitory for students to live on campus. That was a big opportunity for me. I got the extra money together and moved from Dad's house. For the first time in my life, I felt free. I had a very strong sense that living on campus would support me in winning the academic battle. Basil, who was doing very well academically, must have had the same idea. He moved to campus and became my roommate. There was no cafeteria in the dorm but Basil and I got dishwashing jobs in the school cafeteria.

A short time after school started, we noticed that the mysterious Mr. John Green was missing. John was nowhere around. No one had a clue about where he'd gone. Maybe he had gone back into the Air Force. No one knew. Soon, we gave up and just stopped wondering where he had gone.

I was a sophomore and still pursuing the stupid idea of majoring in Chemistry. Based on some bad advice, I took an advanced level Chemistry course called Quantitative Analysis. Usually, third year Chemistry majors took this course that was 50% laboratory work and 50% lecture. Most of the time in this class, I had no clue what was going on.

The idea of this kind of chemistry is that you take a sample and figure out how much of each chemical element there is in the sample. This meant using balance scales that were sensitive enough to weigh a single human hair. The slightest miscalculation would throw your lab results completely off. You had to be accurate to the third decimal place. I had never been that accurate before or since that class about anything. The professor was very kind to me. He gave me a "D" instead of an "F." Since this was a four-credit course, it had a heavy impact on my grade point average. That grade sank my Chemistry aspirations as well as my chances for a scholarship for the second semester.

This whole incident forced me to make a new decision about choosing a major. I looked around to see the courses in which I was doing well and decided to major in Mathematics. Actually, my reasoning was that I would take math courses until I flunked out then I would change to another major. Later, in 1957, when the Russians launched the first spacecraft, Sputnik, it seemed that I had made the right choice. Because, all the media were saying that the country had to stress science and science-related knowledge. So, with a degree in math, I thought I had a good chance of getting a decent job.

That was also the year of a momentus shift in KCU's policy about its image and future growth as well as, coincidentally, my future. For years, KCU had struggled with the problem of attracting more students. Most Kansas City kids were like me, they wanted to go away to college. If "going away" only meant going to Missouri University (MU), about 90 miles east of Kansas City, in Columbia, Missouri.

MU offered a good athletic program that provided not only athletic scholarships, but a big league way for Friday night high school heroes to continue their quests for glory. Big time athletics offered students the chance for more partying and a broader range of extra curricula activities.

Seeing this drain on the potential student pool, the KCU administration was forced to shift their policy to include intercollegiate athletics. Adding this layer of athletics seemed to be a solution to KCU's growth problems.

Later, this policy shift had a major effect on my career at KCU.

Eventually it made the difference in my finishing my education at KCU versus having to complete it at some other school.

All during high school, I had wanted to go out for a sport. Since I had had a bad experience with the basketball jocks clique, track was a last resort. However, I never actually tried out for the high school track team. In spite of this, I was always sure that I could run fast. In the fall of 1956, the KCU Athletic department hired its first track coach. The new coach, Fred Beile, wasn't sure about my running ability but he told me that I could go to the National Small College track meet in San Diego, California, in June if I could throw the javelin 150 feet. That was all the incentive I needed to sign up. Since the coach was desperate for warm bodies to field some kind of a track team, he encouraged me to try out for the team. Lack of experience was not a problem. Anyone that showed up was very likely to make the team. With no past track record, I was instantly on the KCU varsity track team.

We started training in early January. I was so excited about being on the track team that I talked my roommate Basil North into joining the team. Those of us who went out for track were nervous about mentioning that fact in class. Being an athlete was not popular on campus yet. The University had such a strong academic bias that we felt there was a stigma associated with being an athlete.

At the beginning of the season in March, a number of former high school track stars showed up. After the first mid-term exams, we lost half of those "would-be" team members. That left us with a small, hardcore team of mostly inexperienced "want-to-bes." Initially, my focus was on throwing the javelin so I could go to San Diego at the end of the season. As the season got underway, Coach Beile asked me to try some other running events. I had no real knowledge of what I was doing. Coach Beile had been a nationally recognized middle distance (half-mile and mile) runner at Southern Illinois University. He was not much help in the sprints towards which I gravitated. I had to depend on my natural ability and occasional coaching from my more experienced teammates. As the season developed, I did other events and gained some proficiency in a few. On a typical day, I would run the 100 yard dash, broad jump (now called the long jump), throw the javelin, run the 220 yard dash and run a leg on the mile relay (440 yards). Later, I added running a leg on the 880-yard relay (220 yards).

While the 100-yard dash was my favorite event, that first year I would usually come in second. Mid-way through the season, I developed a pulled thigh muscle. It plagued me the rest of the season. Before every track meet, I would have to have my leg taped.

The Lean Mean Running Machine
Me -- Glaring out of the starting blocks on a typical day on the track. Note the superb fitness and svelte, athletic body.

I am very fortunate to have gotten a great education at KCU. At age eighteen, I learned to think. I took Economics 101. That was the turning point in my education and, subsequently, my life. I didn't learn much about Economics, but I did learn to think critically and to synthesize data from multiple sources. Dr. Earl Smith, a brilliant and somewhat eccentric professor, taught this "Economics" course. My buddy Basil and I took the course together.

The first day of class, Professor Smith said, "None of you have PhDs; therefore you are not smart enough to create anything." I could feel the entire room full of students recoil. Having achieved his desired affect, Dr. Smith said, "If you want to make an "A" in this course, you will do the following three things. This statement perked us up a bit. We couldn't remember any teacher up to that point telling us how to make an "A." We were all ears.

"First," Dr. Smith said, "You must take verbatim notes on everything I say." There were a few groans from the group. Then he continued. "Secondly, at final examination time, you will write in your exam booklets everything I have said during the course without referring to your notes." Hushed silence fell upon the room.

One brave soul raised his hand and asked, "You want us to regurgitate everything you said?"

"That is exactly what I want you to do." Dr. Smith said. He finished by saying: "Finally, I don't give many A's, but those who get them stay in the exam room for a minimum of six hours. One of my students stayed twelve hours. The standard three hours, usually set aside for final exams, will not be enough time. You will be on the honor system, which means that no one will be there to make sure you don't use your notes. Therefore, you can stay as long as you feel you have to."

One student, who was unfamiliar with the honor system, raised her hand. "Dr. Smith." She said, "What if someone uses their notes?"

"You have a moral obligation to tell me." Dr. Smith said. "Besides, I have spies everywhere. So, we could catch any cheaters. And, I have other ways of knowing."

When we got back to the dorm, Basil and I had a field day talking about this dude. Where did they get this crazy, S.O.B.? Then we went on to talk about his short legs, which we thought probably equated to his short penis, and we spent some time speculating about his lineage. In spite of his weirdness, we knew this guy was serious and we had better not mess with him. It never occurred to us to drop that class as about one-third of the first day's attendees did.

Economics 101 started with a discussion of folkways and mores. He lectured on how folkways and mores affected the fundamental problem of economics -- how to distribute limited means among an unlimited set of competing ends. We looked at the underpinnings of a society that encouraged little old ladies to drive huge Cadillacs, burning gallons and gallons of gas, when they could drive Volkswagen Beetles.

It is funny how you have to understand something well in order to commit it to memory. Basil and I rose to the occasion. Somehow, Dr. Smith had put the fear of God into us, so looking at our notebooks was not an option. He had convinced us that he would know if we violated the honor code and there would be dire consequences, such as being expelled from the University. Although Dr. Smith professed not to believe in God, he knew how to put the fear of God into us. Both Basil and I got a B in this course. I think we stayed in the exam room about six hours each.

In retrospect, this course had a magical effect on Basil and me for the rest of our lives. Basil, who later became a highly successful attorney and I, who enjoyed a successful foray into corporate America, owe much of that success to the eccentric Dr. Smith. Through the professor's slow, comprehensive dismantling of everything we held sacred (including God) we had the rug pulled out from under our minds. That left us with the urgent need to rebuild our philosophical infrastructures starting from zero. We had to carefully examine our previously unexamined sacred cows. Once one learns to think, the limitations fall away. This brief encounter with a true intellectual was a life altering experience. It was as if we were thrown into a sea of intellect and had to learn to swim.

CHAPTER **17**

The Summer in L A

AT ONE TRACK meet, I managed to throw the javelin 152 feet. The Coach kept his word. He entered my teammate, Bill Nickel, and me, in the National Small College track meet held in San Diego. Bill's father had just given Bill a new Ford sedan, which we drove from Kansas City to San Diego in June 1957. The trip took about three days. The drive to San Diego was an exciting event. To my shock and awe, Bill pushed the car up to 100 MPH and left it there for long distances. We stopped for gas when we got to the middle of Kansas. Bill and I got out, stretched our legs and filled the tank. When it was time to go, Bill jumped in the car on the passenger side and ordered me to drive for the next shift.

"Oh no, Bill, I can't drive. I don't have a driver's license." I said.

"Well I guess we'll just have to sit here." Bill said, resolutely, as he folded his arms.

After a brief standoff, I said, "What the hell! I guess I'll have to drive?" I got behind the wheel and we took off. After about ten minutes, Bill leaned over and while looking at the speedometer, he said, "You're going pretty goddamned slow."

"But I'm going seventy, the speed limit."

"You got to pick it up or it will take us a week to get to San Diego."

Easing the speedometer up to 105 MPH, I said, "Okay Chief, you got it."

After that, we both kept the speed around 100 all the way across the country. Somewhere out in the middle of New Mexico, we barely missed a rattlesnake or something that was crossing the road. Thankfully, it got across the road before we hit it. There was no way we could have stopped if we had hit it. We would have been splattered all over the highway, if we hadn't missed it.

The absolute scariest part of the trip was when we drove through the mountains just outside Flagstaff, Arizona. It was Bill's turn to drive. He kept it under 100, but not by much. Seeing all of the little white crosses that marked where people had gone off the edge of the road was a sobering experience. At several points, there were five or six crosses in memory of multiple victims. The only way I got through this drive was to close my eyes most of the time until we were out of the mountains.

The track meet was at night. I took a couple of javelin throws, but didn't come close to getting into the finals. I ran one of the heats in the 100-yard dash, but again, I didn't qualify for the finals. In spite of my poor performance, the experience of being in the same track meet with the country's top small college track athletes was well worth the harrowing drive.

A few days later Bill dropped me off at my Mom's place and I was ready to begin my summer in LA. I was fortunate enough to get a job for the summer. This was my summer of lost innocence, which included an affair with a married woman. Although I felt like some kind of moral retard, my surging hormones eventually forgave that dalliance. After the hormones subsided a bit, I was able to rationalize my behavior by saying that this was life in LA.

One day during that summer, an astonishing thing happened. I was on the way home after having spent the day hanging out with my married lady friend. I was standing in the safety zone waiting for a streetcar. A streetcar came up, but it was the wrong one so I stayed in the safety zone. As it passed, I saw this face looking out from the rear of the streetcar. In a split second, we both recognized each other. It was John Green! Before either of us could say anything or exchange phone numbers, the streetcar roared away. Although it was two years before I saw him again, at least I could solve the John Green mystery for everyone back at KCU.

With the exception of the "B" I received in Economics 101, my grades were marginal during the second semester of my second year in school. It did not look like my scholarship would be renewed for the third year. During the summer, I wrote several letters to Basil, my buddy, explaining my plan to live in LA rather than come back to school at KCU. I started thinking in terms of keeping my job as a warehouse-receiving clerk and figuring out a way to go to school at night.

Late in the summer, I received a letter from Basil containing some great news! The University had changed its scholarship requirements from strictly academics to include financial need. Because of this change, I ended up getting a much bigger scholarship renewal in spite of my grades. I was able to return to KCU in September 1957. I suspect that my efforts at track during the previous Spring may have been a significant factor.

His father bought him a car during the summer, so it was easier for Basil to commute from home, and he decided not to move back into the dorm. Because of my situation at home, I declared myself emancipated at age twenty. I made the dorm my permanent home and I never gave any thought to living in my father's house again. His house became no more than a way station. Victor Battle, a Black fellow from St. Louis, replaced Basil as my roommate. Victor was a Pharmacy major.

The first semester of my junior year at KCU was very grim academically. I made all "C"s. This fact was terribly depressing. The most depressing part was that I had little or no social life and spent most of my time in the library studying to make "C's" in everything. To me, a 1.0 grade point average meant I was a total failure. For several days, I sat around the dorm thinking, *"I would much rather be out in the streets, driving fast cars and chasing girls."* I concluded that I was doing this whole college trip to please my Dad and other people.

Also, there were very few people in my family that ever graduated from college. Following that train of logic, there didn't seem to be any good reasons to stay in school. The whole idea of school seemed pointless. It was a dilemma, I didn't want to stay and I couldn't leave. I was between a rock and a hard place. I worked myself into such a snit that I decided that I needed to talk to someone before I dropped out or did something equally stupid.

I surfaced from the depression long enough to make an appointment with one of the dorm counselors. The guy I chose was a second year dental student named Ed Lamb. Seeking out someone to talk to was one of the smartest things I ever did. We talked non-stop for about four hours. I explained my disillusionment with school, my life, and everything else. I told him I couldn't see any point in continuing school. He was very understanding. He suggested that I try thinking about self-satisfaction as a reason to complete school. He convinced me that I could do it for myself and that would be enough. I came out of that meeting with a new sense of personal purpose and determination. Thanks to Ed Lamb, the dorm counselor, I was empowered to push ahead just for my own personal satisfaction of completing college. I could have the satisfaction of completing something I had started.

By now, I was a full-blown math major, taking advanced math courses. The second semester improved and school became easier to handle. One day I started working on an Advanced Calculus proof involving partial differential equations. I was following the proof as outlined in the text until I got to a point where several steps had been left out. I worked on this for three or four days, off and on. Finally, one afternoon I closed myself in an empty phone booth in the dorm. I declared that I was not coming out of that phone booth until I had solved the problem. About three hours later, I arrived at the insight needed to complete the proof. This experience made me feel like a big time mathematician.

About a week later, my roommate, Victor, got an eye exam and some glasses. He told me that they really helped. That seemed like a good idea. I had never considered the possibility that I might need glasses. With my last few dollars, I got some reading glasses. The results were amazing. My grades improved dramatically. In most of the classes in which I was making "C"s, I began making "A"s or "B"s with very little additional effort. For the first time since I had been in college, I was able to read for more than fifteen minutes without falling asleep. The new reading glasses allowed me to get through an entire chapter of whatever I was studying, such as World History, American History, etc. I could read for hours without falling asleep. Being able to read a full chapter meant I could actually remember what I had read. For as long as I could remember, it seems I had been suffering eyestrain from reading. After fifteen minutes, my eyes and my mind would shut down. Assuming that I was sleepy, I would take a little nap. When I awoke and tried again, I had the same result. That is one definition of insanity -- doing the same thing expecting a different result.

While I was struggling academically, I ran on the cross-country track team during the Fall season. The idea was to strengthen my leg muscles in time for the Spring track season. Practice for running cross-country consisted of five individual one-mile wind sprints followed by thirty minutes of up-hill running. The competitive events involved running three to four miles over a golf course or a meadow. I usually came in last but eventually, all of this pain and humiliation paid off.

By the Spring track season, my legs were much stronger than in the previous year and I had an amazing season. In order to get some public relations for the University, Coach Beile arranged to have the core track team members appear on one of the local TV stations. During the beginning of the sports segment of the evening news, the team lined up in a row across the studio and when the camera panned on each of us, we were to give our name, our track event and our class rank. While I generally had very little contact with my family, I did call them and tell them that I was going to be on TV.

I learned years later that my brief appearance on TV had quite an impact at home. Somehow, my little brothers, Donnie and Edward, heard about the upcoming event. I think they really got it when my Dad spent $50 to get their TV fixed so they could watch. As Donnie describes it, "We could hardly believe our eyes. Our big brother was on TV." After he saw the brief clip of me on the evening sports news, he had to spread the word to his second grade classmates.

The next day when he went to school, the trouble started. According to Donnie, "The first words out of my mouth when I got to school were, 'My brother was on TV last night." That is when the argument started. Another little kid said, "No way, your brother wasn't on no TV."

"Yes. He was."

"Was not."

"Was too."

"Was not."

This went on until there was no alternative but to throw some punches at the non-believer and his friends, who were just as steadfast in their disbelief. The non-believers responded with some punches of their own. After a series of pitched battles, my little brother had to walk away with the internal knowledge that he had seen what he had seen, no matter what anyone said. As far as he was concerned, his big brother was a hero that had been on TV and that was the end of it.

CHAPTER 18

Athletics: Front and Center

THE OUTDOOR TRACK season officially started at the end of March. I still ran several events, but this year I placed first most of the time. I lost first place only once or twice during the entire season in meets at the small schools that we competed against.

I became a sort of campus hero. It didn't matter at KCU as far as the girls were concerned. The racial environment in Kansas City and on campus was so stifling and backwards that any White girl that expressed even a passing interest in a Black athlete would be labeled a slut and ostracized from polite society. I got the point one day, when a cute little brunette came out to watch me practice javelin throwing. I noticed her, but never said a word to her. Some guys were watching from the dorm across the street. By the time I finished practice and got back to the dorm, the rumor had spread that this same little brunette had "made it" with the entire basketball team. While I never had a chance to talk to her, I can only imagine that the rumor mill must have made her life a living hell. In spite of this kind of incident, the KCU campus labored under the illusion of being fully integrated.

One afternoon, I added another specialty to my track repertoire. I learned the hop, step and jump event. This event is now called the triple jump. This event is very complex, requiring a great deal of rhythm, balance, and coordination. Bill Nickel, my San Diego buddy, (who coincidentally was a rich white kid) introduced this event to our track team. Bill had been a world-class long jumper, who had been recruited by the University of Southern California (USC). One day he broke both ankles during practice at USC. That ended his track career at USC and he came back home to Kansas City and KCU. Bill was ambitious and picked up the idea that he could go to the Olympics in the triple jump, because it was an event in which most Americans did poorly. The world champion at that time was a Brazilian athlete with the wonderful name of Adhemar da Silva. Adhemar won gold medals in the 1952 and the 1956 Olympics for the triple jump. At his own expense, Bill traveled to the Texas Relays in Austin, Texas, and filmed Mr. Da Silva in action. I watched Bill frequently in practice and decided that the triple jump was too much for me. I was certain that I could not achieve the necessary balance and coordination.

One afternoon, while we were warming up for practice, I started clowning around. I figured that I would try the triple jump, land flat on my face, everyone would have a good laugh and then we would get on with practice. I ran down the field, took a large hop followed by a long step and jumped into the sandpit. To the coach's and my own amazement, I didn't fall flat on my face. The coach came running over and said, "Let's see you do that again." Thinking this was all just a fluke, I laughingly took another jump. The coach got very excited and said, "Let's measure that one!" I had jumped about forty-six feet. The school record, which Bill held, was forty-seven feet. By now, all my teammates had gathered around watching this strange happening. I backed up, took another run and jumped. I had an awesome feeling while floating through the air. It felt like I was never going to come down. This jump measured forty-eight feet, breaking Bill's school record. The coach was elated. He now had two triple jumpers that could compete in the larger, regional track meets at the big schools like Kansas University. I was flabbergasted. Actually, I never equaled or exceeded that distance again. Somehow, I was never able to be that loose or relaxed once I got serious about being a triple jumper. Bill did go on to get the school record back with a jump of forty-nine feet the following year at the Drake Relays. I also had a fantastic day with the triple jump at that meet.

Mom invited me to spend the summer in LA. Before I could go, I had to help Dad dig a swimming pool in the backyard of some rich white folks, to earn train fare to LA. It was an awful job. We started the job with the idea of digging most of the pool with our small tractor. The backyard where we were digging was so confined that we could only dig half of the pool using the tractor. We had to dig the rest by hand. The casual wino laborers we hired for part of the project failed to show up so Dad and I had to finish the job ourselves. We had a dump truck that we drove up as close as we could get to one side of the hole. Each shovel of dirt had to be thrown up out of the five-foot hole and over the four foot height of the dump truck side panels. There were times when I felt like John Henry, "Swinging a nine pound hammer ...." The entire process was backbreaking and slow. We would fill up the dump truck and drive it out into the country to dump the dirt. Then we would have to come back and do it all over again. I was very tired and sore by the time I got on the train to LA, but it was worth it.

I came back to school in the fall of 1958 (my senior year) on a full scholarship with extra money to buy books. By now, it was sort of an athletic scholarship. I had a great indoor track season that fall. It started at the University of Chicago, then the University of Omaha and then a little podunk school, Marshal College in Marshal, Missouri. Kansas State University was the last meet of the indoor track circuit for us.

In mid-December, the track coach decided that we should go to the University of Chicago for an indoor track meet. This event, called the Knights of Columbus Indoor Track Meet, took place annually on the 27th of December. The coach and three of us tracksters, piled into a University station wagon on Christmas Day and drove to Chicago. We stopped at a little diner for Christmas dinner in some little Podunk Iowa town. I felt quite sad, because this was the first Christmas I was ever away from home. The coach booked us cheap rooms at the Chicago YMCA on Wabash Ave. Some homeless guys tried to help us into the building so they could get warm. The YMCA staff made a big deal out of rushing the homeless guys out of the lobby and back onto the streets. Outside on the streets, the snow had partially melted and it was covered with soot and ashes. In those days, instead of putting sand on snow and ice, the cities used ashes. That was my first impression of Chicago -- cold and very, very dirty.

The coach had signed me up for the 60-yard dash. A large number of schools participated in the meet so the race had to be divided into several preliminary runs or so-called heats. The first and second place finishers of each heat qualified to run in the final race. Ira Murchison, a short stocky guy with huge, bulging leg muscles, who was the current holder of the world's record in the 100-yard dash, settled into the lane next to me during one of the preliminary heats. By the time I raised up to come out of the starting blocks, Murchison and some other dude were breaking the tape for the finish. I readily accepted the fact that I didn't have a chance against this kind of world class competition. My consolation was that at least I had been in the same heat. I was not too perturbed. That fact made a very positive impact on the rest of my indoor track season.

With the 60-yard dash out of the way, I went back to my skills in the triple jump. I placed fourth in the triple jump overall competition and Bill took second. That almost justified our trip to Chicago.

Although we weren't supposed to, my teammates and I got together and walked down the street from the Y. We found a tiny "hole-in-the-wall" bar. It turned out to be a rip-off place. Beers were $5 each (an unheard of price during the fifty's) and the woman dancing on a platform behind the bar, seemed to end up with more clothes on than she started with. Our big night out in Chicago only added to my negative view of the city.

On our way out of Chicago, the next day -- Sunday morning -- we stopped at a corner for a traffic light. Two Black hookers that looked like they each weighed 300 pounds, with skirts practically up to their navels, acted as if they wanted to jump into our station wagon. As horny as I was, I felt a great sense of relief when the coach sped away. A few blocks later, as we went through an intersection, a motorcycle cop pulled us over.

"License and registration please." The officer said.

"Yes, sir." The coach said, as he handed the documents out the window.

"Do you know you ran a red light two blocks back?" The officer asked with an accusing tone.

"No, Officer, I wasn't aware of running a red light." Coach said firmly.

"Well, it looks like I'm going to have to take you guys down to the precinct." The officer said, matter-of-factly.

Coach Beile, who had been to Chicago before, stared back at the officer stoically while saying, "Well officer, I guess you'll have to take us to the station."

The officer hemmed and hawed for a minute. Then he stammered a bit out of frustration. Then, finally after a long pregnant silence the officer said, "Well seeing as how it says on your station wagon that you're from the University of Kansas City, I'm going to make an exception and let you guys go on back to Kansas City."

"Thanks, Officer." Coach Beile said, as we drove away.

A few miles down the road, Coach explained that this whole incident with the cop had been a request for a bribe and he had called the cop's bluff. This blatant incident solidified all my negative impressions and I wrote Chicago off as a city to which I would ever return. It took many years and several business trips for me to discover Chicago's rich blues tradition and to turn around my youthful negativity.

Three weekends later, we drove to the University of Omaha for a twelve-school indoor track meet. That meet included several smaller schools from around the Midwest such as Mankato State, Graceland, Beloit, etc. I remember sitting in the dressing room thinking about the meet. All of a sudden, a remarkable attitude came over me. I thought, *"Three weeks ago I was running against Ira Murchison, a world record holder, and now here I am in Omaha, Nebraska running against a bunch of country bumpkins."* I copped an attitude like. *"These guys can't carry my jock."* I strode out onto the track for the first 60-yard preliminary heat. I was dripping with attitude. When the gun went off for the start of the race, I drove out of the starting blocks and never looked back. It seemed like only a few strides before the tape hit me in the chest. I had won that heat by about five yards. The coach came running up clicking his stopwatch and shouting, "Do you know what you just did?" I had no clue, but I was feeling pretty loose. I had run the 60-yard dash in a very respectable 6.4 seconds. It was respectable enough to establish a new field house record at the University of Omaha. I ran the final race in the same time, after three unnerving, false starts. The coach was overjoyed. I felt as if I had arrived as a viable track athlete.

Marshal College was the next leg of the indoor campaign. Marshal was a tiny college in central Missouri. This was KCU's second invitation to Marshal. This year, they put in an unexpected wrinkle. In addition to KCU, Marshal invited Lincoln University, an all Black school located in Jefferson City, Missouri. I was scared to death. My own subtle racism rose to the surface. I was reasonably confident that I could easily beat most of the White runners, but these Black runners were a different story.

With the exception of Murchison at the Chicago meet, I had not run against many Black guys. They looked serious and tough enough to kick my butt. I spent almost an hour warming up. I wanted to be sure that I was ready. I didn't want to be written off as some little "Uncle Tom" dude running for the "Massa," holding up the rich white folk's banner. We ran the first heat and there was no one around at the end but the tape and me. That felt damned good. Maybe I had a chance with these dudes. In the final race, I set a field house record for that school. I ran a very respectable 6.3 seconds for the 60-yard dash. I felt like I had come into my own as a competitive sprinter. Whatever the Lincoln U. guys thought of me, they at least had to admit that I was a fast "Uncle Tom."

An indoor track meet at Kansas State University in Manhattan Kansas was the last leg of the indoor season. Somehow, I allowed myself to be intimidated by the big time sprinters from Kansas, Oklahoma and Texas Universities. I ran a respectable 6.3 seconds for the 60 yard dash. In that crowd it took a 6.2 or a 6.1 to have a chance. I had to be satisfied with my previous dominance of the small schools.

The spring track season was as successful as the indoor season had been. I could consistently run a 9.8-second 100-yard dash. In my small college league, any time under 10-seconds flat was outstanding. The big guys over at Kansas University were running 9.5 second 100-yard dashes, so I wasn't that bad. Often, because I was running several other events during a two-school meet, I learned to lay back. I learned to run to win rather than set a record or push myself unnecessarily.

Because I was on the track team, I was assured of eating better. Going to a track meet was like a party. The food was good before and after the meet. The coach used to kid me about loading up on pancakes, sausage, and eggs at breakfast on the way to track meets. Coach Beile really appreciated us hardcore track team members. That is why he had a policy of feeding us well no matter how we did on the track. Whether we won or lost, we always had a great breakfast (or lunch) and steak for dinner. As my Dad would say, this was like "shitting in high cotton."

Because the team was very small, the coach scheduled us for the larger regional meets. While driving to the meets, Coach, who valued each of us highly as individuals, would sometimes complain about the fact that most of us were Math or Engineering majors. "Why couldn't I get some regular guys, instead of you nerds?" he would sometimes ask rhetorically. He would fain total exasperation when we would start discussing a problem in differential equations while on the way to a meet.

At these large regional meets, we could focus on our individual specialties and not worry so much about the overall team score. I started seriously doing the triple jump (or the hop, step, and jump, as it was called in those days). The series of large regional track meets included such meets as the Kansas Relays, the Drake Relays and the Beloit Relays. The Drake Relays was the crown jewel of the large regional, multi-school meets. It was a prestigious meet held at Drake

University in Des Moines, Iowa. The whole town seemed to be involved in the meet. Everywhere we went people seemed to go out of their way to welcome us to their town and to the meet.

Coincidentally, the spring of 1959 was the 50th anniversary of this meet and the whole city of Des Moines went all out for this event. All the champion athletes who had run at Drake in the previous fifty years were honored in a special ceremony. What a thrilling event that was. I even got Jesse Owens to autograph my program as he passed through the locker room. That was one of the greatest moments of my entire athletic career.

There was another miraculous moment for me at this meet. I ran a heat of the 100-yard dash just to say I had run against some big guns. Two or three of the sprinters in my heat had equaled the world record the week before. The triple jump however, was my main event. My friend Bill Nickel and I thought we could take first and second. Each person had four preliminary jumps to get into the final competition. On my first two jumps, I had roared down the approach, and fouled by stepping over the line before I jumped. The next jump was a disappointing thirty-eight feet, which was hardly good enough to get into the finals. At this point, I was trying not to panic. I had one more jump to make it into the finals. As I started to run down the approach to take the last jump, I decided to let it all hang out. The distance was only forty-three feet. I just knew I had not qualified for the finals.

I walked over into the center of the track and took off my shoes. I was feeling awful. I didn't see how I could face the Coach or my teammates. Then I heard my name called. I had made the finals after all. I hurriedly put on my shoes and ran over to the triple jump area. This jump was only slightly better than the 38-foot jump. On the next try, I fouled. Finally, on my last jump, I let it all hang out. The distance was forty-four feet, six and one-half inches. This distance was a tie for fourth place, which was the last place that received a medal. Since there was only one medal, I had to toss a coin with the other guy. Miraculously, I won the coin toss and the medal. I could hardly believe what an incredible day this had been. I was thrilled to win any kind of medal at such a prestigious track meet. That fourth place medal is still one of my proudest possessions.

The Beloit Relays was our final major multi-school track meet. Beloit, Wisconsin is a small town in Southern Wisconsin a few miles north of Rockford, Illinois and the Illinois border. The town was built around the college, which was founded before Wisconsin became a state. With its 1,100 students, the college was the centerpiece of the town. The Beloit Relays hosted most of the small colleges in the Midwest and upper Midwest regions. This multi-school track meet was one of the town's biggest events. The meet was set up so that during the first two days, all of the preliminary events were run. The final events were held on the third night of the competition under the Beloit college stadium lights.

After the meet, a downtown restaurant owner closed his place to other customers and invited all of the athletes for an incredible T-bone steak dinner. The T-bone steaks were so large that they covered the entire huge plate on which they were served. Since this was the last meet of the season, the beer flowed freely and the coaches looked the other way. By this point in the season, I was fairly wiped out and was more focused on graduating, so I don't remember doing very well at this meet. Nevertheless, I do remember the sumptuous T-bone steak dinner and the pitchers of great Wisconsin beer.

CHAPTER **19**

Academic Resurgence

IN ADDITION TO my track escapades, I did very well academically in my senior year at KCU. I made "A's" and "B's" consistently, with the exception of an advanced math course called Vector Analysis. The Vector Analysis Professor was German and his accent was so thick that he was embarrassed himself by it. He was so embarrassed that he would go to the board and start working on an example problem the minute class started. Without explaining what he was doing, he would grunt his way through an hour or so of laborious problem solving on the board. After a while, I stopped going to class and got tutoring from a friend who would help me enough to barely pass the tests when they came up. The professor was kind and gave me a "D" rather than an "F." That turned out to be the critical grade I needed to graduate.

Other than the fact that I had bought into the propaganda that any science or science-related degree would be a gold mine as far as a job was concerned, I had no clue what I would do with a math degree. Teaching seemed like a good place to start. So, I began taking courses in the Education Department, because I thought it would be a good idea to have a teaching certificate as backup. I took all the education courses required to get a certificate, except the Practice Teaching Course. I figured I could do that later. I was thrilled when the Professor of Educational Psychology asked to keep a copy of the final paper

I wrote about my theory that maturity and struggle were critical to the successful learning of Mathematics. There was another important Education course called Contemporary Education. The professor, Dr. Levin, was so frustrated by the light content of this "required" course, that he added a segment on critical thinking. This course was the crown jewel of the great education that I received at KCU.

During College, my social life was very Spartan. My dalliance with the married lady in LA was the high point of my social life. During my last year at KCU, somehow I fell into a strange, platonic courtship with Dorothy Lockett. Dorothy lived in my neighborhood -- Leeds. She played piano and taught Sunday school at the church to which I belonged. She was about three years older than I was. All through high school, I had a mild crush on her but neither of us took it seriously.

When I had bus fare, I would go to church in my old neighborhood where Dorothy still played the piano. After church, I had a standing invitation to her house for Sunday afternoon dinner. Her parents began counting on me to do something serious. At one point, I touched Dorothy on the knee. Both of us were shocked. I had put her on such a high pedestal that I couldn't imagine kissing her or being intimate with her in any way. In spite of this almost platonic relationship, we developed an unspoken promise that one day we would probably marry. So, most of my last year in college, we had hot and heavy hand holding dates. After those Sunday afternoon dates, I never walked the few blocks to my Dad's house. I would get on the bus for school without looking back.

Graduation day was on Sunday, May 31, 1959. I received a bachelor's degree in Mathematics, with all the rights and privileges pursuant thereto. I was ready. I was so tired of eating potted meat and crackers. I wanted a real life. Knowing that I had very limited prospects for a meaningful job in Kansas City, because of the racial climate, my first thought was to go to Los Angeles. Unlike my Granddad, who had made that trek in the early 40's, I felt that my education gave me a much better chance.

The only way to get to LA was to earn the train fare. I was too independent to ask Mom, Dad or anyone else for help. The result was that I had to swallow my pride and go to work for my Dad to earn my train fare. After a backbreaking week of manual labor that I wasn't accustomed to, Dad made some lame excuse about using my earnings to meet that week's payroll. Suspecting that this was some kind of ploy to keep me around, I made it clear to him that that couldn't happen again. I also made sure that he understood that I was going to LA if I had to hitch hike. I think he got the message and didn't screw around with my pay the following week.

I got a ticket and was out of there on the slow train to LA.

CHAPTER **20**

Down and Almost Out in Los Angeles

WHILE I WAS surprised to find no employers waiting, it was a great feeling to step off the train at LA's Union Station in the June sunshine. I felt certain that getting a job would be no problem. I was counting on the lady who had previously helped me get a summer job. She was someone Granddad had worked for when he was in the horse handling business. The fact that her employment agency was located in the center of downtown LA convinced me that this job finding thing was going to be a piece of cake. Ha!!

I went on interview after interview and took test after test, but there was no job. I began to be increasingly depressed. One day I was so depressed, that I looked over the edge of a high bridge and had some very disturbing thoughts. The excuse I heard most often was, "We don't want to hire you, train you, and then have you get drafted." Apparently, it was some combination of discrimination and the recession.

I lived with my Mom during this dreadful period. She was very kind and understanding. After six months of bone-crushing unemployment, I started getting desperate and panicky. The situation took a significant toll on my self-esteem.

Mom's apartment was only about ten blocks from the University of Southern California (USC) campus. One day while looking around the campus for a library that I could use without being a student, I ran into John Green as he was leaving the campus. We were both just as shocked as we had been during our brief streetcar encounter a few years earlier. The difference this time was that we had time to chat and exchange phone numbers.

Along the way, I reached the conclusion that joining the California National Guard was one way of handling the "you'll get drafted" excuse. This move would also help me avoid being drafted. To keep my sanity before going away to the Army for six months of active duty, I took a job as a dishwasher in a bowling alley restaurant in Santa Monica. I had to get up every morning at 5 AM and catch a bus for the two-hour ride to Santa Monica. I worked at the bowling alley about three months. Then I was off to the Army for six-months of active duty at Fort Ord, in Northern California.

One day, in the middle of basic training, I got a letter from Kansas City bearing the news that Dorothy Lockett had married some minister. Getting up at 5 AM every morning, and doing four or five mile hikes in full combat gear didn't leave much time for feeling devastated about being jilted. It didn't take long for me to realize that I couldn't consider myself jilted if I only had an unspoken engagement.

After six weeks in Basic Training, I spent the next six weeks in Army Clerk School. About 50% of the training time was about learning to type. I was such a bad typist that I only qualified for the position of "Clerk, General" That was the Army's way of saying, "This is a soldier who can't type, so he is only a clerk." On the brighter side, Clerk School was in the same area as the Cook School and we ate in their dining room (or mess hall). During that six weeks of clerk training, I ate very well. Thanksgiving arrived and I was depressed about not having enough time to go home to LA. I felt quite gloomy until I walked into the dining room and saw the most fantastic Thanksgiving spread I had ever seen. Not only was there turkey with all the trimmings and side dishes of vegetables, but the place was decorated with a fall, harvest theme. It was absolutely beautiful.

After being away in the Army for six months, I came back to LA and found a $50 a week clerk job. I lied about my college background to get this job. I told them I had completed only two years of college and that I was still going to school. I was also fortunate enough to not take a required typing test -- which I would have failed. The lady who administered the test was sick on the day I went for my final interview.

It was 1960. John Green was finishing school at USC and getting ready to marry Patsy Hall, his fiancée from Kansas City. John introduced me to his old Air Force buddy, Henry Dock -- "Dock." John, Dock and I made the most of our bachelor days. Dock was going to UCLA and we went to many impromptu parties with his UCLA basketball friends. Dock also knew several girls whose apartments we would go to in the middle of the night armed with a six-pack and a bottle of Ripple or Thunderbird wine. Once we arrived, we'd start the party. LA was relatively sane in those days and we could walk all over the central city at 4 AM in the morning without a hassle.

Sometimes, we would get a six-pack and find a park. We would drink the six-pack and then head for the Dodgers' game. In those days, the Dodgers had just come to LA. They were playing in the LA Coliseum just across from the USC campus. We would slip into the game about the seventh inning. Dock, John, and I would make more noise than the paying fans. We had a good, cheap form of entertainment that lasted until John got married. Instead of the park, we could now take our six-pack to John and Pat's apartment.

At this point, I had been working at my $50/week clerk job for about nine months. One of those months included a Memorial Day Monday. I got together with my buddy Dock and one of his friends, who had a car. Being a married man, John couldn't run around with us anymore. We cruised around LA looking for girls to pick up. One of our crew picked up an old girl friend. With no women for us, Dock and I focused on getting drunk. We drove from one liquor store to the next. We drank beer, malt liquor and finally some bourbon. We went to several peoples' houses looking for a party, but couldn't find one. It was about 4 AM when they dropped me off at home. The next morning I was up at 7 AM ready, more or less, to go to work.

To get to my clerk job, I had to take two streetcars and a bus. That particular morning commute was a trip right out of a bad nightmare. The first streetcar, which was an old style one, rocked back and forth like a boat. Environmentally, the inside of the streetcar was unbelievable. I had never noticed that there were so many varieties of cheap perfume. It seemed that the Black community had cornered the market on cheap perfume and the women on this streetcar were well stocked. I pushed my way to the back door of the streetcar, so I could jump off if I needed to throw up. It was a very rocky ride. I was surprised that I made it to the next streetcar without throwing up. When I got on the second streetcar, I noticed that the cheap perfume people had also blanketed the Mexican community. I took up the same position by the back door but didn't need to use it. After a short bus ride, I was able to run in the door at work just in time to punch my time card at 8 AM.

I invoiced the Sears stores that were major customers for the seat covers we manufactured. My job was to fold the invoices, type the store addresses on an envelope and stack it on the pile for mailing. My office was a little open-ended sort of hallway with a table on which I worked. The boss, Mr. Floom, would walk through about every thirty minutes to make sure I wasn't goofing off.

On this particular day, I did okay until about 10 AM when my hangover hit in full force. Knowing that I could never make it to the bathroom and that Mr. Floom would be making his rounds, I opened the window behind me and let go. I figured that while this foul discharge was flying from two stories up, the stuff would dissipate in the air. It seemed that Mr. Floom had just passed through my office, each time I had to throw up. It was a small miracle that Mr. Floom missed my hangover emissions. By lunch time, I got brave enough to go outside to the lunch wagon that passed through the neighborhood. I looked up at my office window. It wasn't very hard to find. There was a stream of liquid oozing down the side of the building. Still too sick to laugh, I thought that was the funniest thing I had ever seen. I don't think Mr. Floom ever knew what happened. About a month later, I received a raise to $52.50 per week.

That summer, my long-term friends, John and Patsy Green introduced me to Dolores Long. I kept complaining to Pat about not being able to find a woman to date. After two tries, Pat finally suggested that maybe I would want to meet one of her co-workers who wanted to be a lawyer. I was instantly intrigued with the idea of meeting her. The other two dates had been with LA teenyboppers who were very pretty but into material stuff -- what kind of car I had and the kind of clothes I wore. Since I had no car and I was still wearing clothes left over from my college days, I was doomed from the get-go.

We set the date up for three couples to go to Santa Monica beach. When we got to the beach, I put down the letter blanket I had won for my track exploits at KCU. I thought it would impress Dolores. At this stage of my life, I was very shy and scared about this date not working out. After getting Dolores settled on my blanket with the other women, I ran off with the guys splashing in the surf and tossing a football. Every so often, I would check in, and then go back to hanging with the fellows.

About three days later, I got a call from Dolores with a rather strange question. She asked if I was gay, since I had spent so little time with her at the beach. The question shocked me but I reassured her that I wasn't gay. We set up a dinner date for the weekend. This gave me a chance to find out more about this woman. Dolores was about 5'2' with very smooth caramel colored skin. She had a petite, compact figure that made her very attractive. She grew up in a ghetto in Brooklyn, New York called Bedford Sty. She came to LA on her own to find work. I found out later that when she was eighteen, her mother took her latchkey away and refused to let Dolores back into the apartment until she found a job. Shortly after that, Dolores decided to move to LA.

For a while, with headshots in hand, Dolores pursued an acting career. She was so bitten by the idea that she enrolled in the Theater Arts Department at UCLA. By the time I met her, she had switched to the dream of becoming a lawyer, but decided to finish her Theater Arts degree. Dolores was making it happen by working full time at night and going to UCLA during the day. I had never met anyone who was so driven.

I thoroughly admired Dolores and thought she was the brightest, bravest person I had ever met. I could not imagine her coming to LA without knowing a soul and establishing herself. Her passion and determination to succeed completely captivated me.

Since she had a car, it was easier for us to date. We went out a couple more times before she went back to New York on vacation. By now, I was madly in love. I wrote two or three steamy love letters while she was away and got a couple of letters back that gave me some hope that she was starting to feel the same way. The fact that I was underemployed and had no car did not seem to bother her at all. It was difficult to imagine that I had found a woman that loved me just for myself.

Over the summer, our relationship intensified. We started hanging out together on the weekends. We would pick one of the numerous cheap motels in Central LA and spend the weekend making love. I was in seventh heaven, and never felt happier or more fulfilled. Moreover, Dolores was happy too. She had found someone who was trustworthy and who absolutely adored her.

Sometimes during the week, Dolores would pick me up and drive me to her place in Westwood where she was living with some friends. Her old DeSoto sedan had a backseat almost as big as a living room. We would occasionally drive to the beach and make out in her voluminous back seat. That summer of 1960 was one of the most romantic summers of my life. Having read D. H. Lawrence's "Lady Chatterley's Lovers" served me well.

My ambition to succeed in life was cranked up highly by having this lovely woman in my life. That September, I started taking a computer-programming course at LA City College. The cost was only $2.50. That was my inexpensive entrance into the computer business.

Jim Price, one of the people I met at the monthly National Guard Unit meetings, was also trying to avoid the draft. We gravitated toward each other because we were both "College" men. He had only a few more classes to go before graduating from UCLA. Jim was a round-faced, rotund guy who looked like he had stepped right out of a travel brochure for going to Austria to meet German peasants. Jim, who was majoring in psychology, was enamored of science and I questioned whether science had any real relevance, especially psychology. That diversity in thinking set us up for some lively, friendly debates during the otherwise dull National Guard meetings. A real camaraderie grew out of our differences of opinion. He invited me to his house several times to meet his wife, Margie, but I would always find an excuse to decline. The real excuse was that because I was so under employed, I felt that I couldn't keep up with these fast moving UCLA intellectuals.

I stayed in that National Guard Unit because our annual two-week summer camps were near San Francisco. Our unit spent two weeks at Benicia Arsenal about sixty miles east of San Francisco. The first week of our stay was spent getting ready for our weekend pass to San Francisco. When Jim asked if I would like to go to downtown San Francisco with him and Margie, I reluctantly said yes. I put aside my thought that I might end up being a drag on their plans. About an hour later, Margie drove up in a little green sports car and honked for us to come out. I looked out the barracks window and saw her for the first time and I was smitten. It was like a scene out of a movie. All I could see was her incredible, glowing smile and her long, flow-ing, golden hair. I jumped into the little sports car and the three of us headed for San Francisco. We had a wonderful day together. We went to the zoo, the Japanese Tea garden, Chinatown and some of the other tourist attractions in the city.

Even though I was smitten with Margie, I valued and respected Jim's friendship too much to make a move on her. Later, I found out that they had an "open marriage" that made it okay to see other peo-ple. I also surmised, after getting to know Jim better that the open mar-riage was Margie's idea. Jim went along with the open marriage deal to avoid losing her. In any case, that was the beginning of a strange twenty-year relationship. Margie would contrive to get me alone and I would do anything to avoid the slightest hint of impropriety.

About the same time I met Jim, I met another fellow in my National Guard Unit. This was in October 1960. He had overheard me complaining about not being able to get a real job. Three days later, he set up an interview for me at Douglas Aircraft Company (long before it became McDonnell-Douglas).

With my newly found ambition, resulting from meeting Dolores, I got very serious about getting something other than a $50 a week clerk job. Not being sure about the Douglas interview, I created a backup strategy of working at the Post Office at night and going to graduate school during the day. Working at the Post Office seemed like a good approach. So, I went down to the main Post Office and took the Postal Worker's exam. I figured it was worth a shot in spite of the poor success I had had with employment exams. Later, I was surprised to learn that I had passed the exam, and they wanted to hire me.

After a very positive interview at Douglas and another outstanding test performance, it was clear that I had a real shot at the job of Associate Engineer. However, the Douglas hiring process involved a review of my paper work and them making me an employment offer. This process for getting a professional job was completely foreign to me. All of a sudden, I found myself trying to decide between two possible jobs.

While waiting for the decision from Douglas, things started to get sticky. The offer from Douglas seemed to be dragging out. At the same time, the Post Office people started pushing to sign me up. The driving test was the only thing left to do. I scheduled the driving test figuring that I would probably screw it up and would have to re-take it later. This would give me time to hear from Douglas. In spite of my best efforts, I passed the Post Office driving test with flying colors. They gave me some paper work to take back downtown and get me signed up. I had no clue about what to do. The Post Office was working to get me on board by the weekend. I stopped at a phone booth and made a panic call to Douglas Personnel. I got someone on the phone, but she was cagey. The person said, "Mr. Randolph, we will send you a telegram as soon as everything is approved." I was really scared and disappointed. There was no way that I could take a chance on missing both of these jobs. I went back to the main Post Office. The employment clerk made a few notes and then asked if I would come down to be sworn in the next afternoon. I said, "Yes." and I walked out of there with what felt like the burdens of the world on my shoulders.

I got to the nearest phone booth and made another panic call to Douglas. They assured me I would hear one way or the other in two days -- no later then Friday. I called the Post Office the next day and put off my swearing-in until Friday afternoon. Then I went home and sweated bullets. Friday morning came and still no word from Douglas. I made another call to Douglas. This time I wanted some answers. The personnel person hemmed and hawed but I made it clear that I had to have an answer. She finally relented and read the telegram that they were sending. It said, "Dear Mr. Randolph, We are happy to extend to you the position of Associate Engineer at a salary of $490 per month. Please reply with your acceptance as soon as possible." I tried to be cool and not jump through the phone. I was deliriously happy and accepted on the spot. Then I called the Post Office and canceled my swearing in appointment for that afternoon.

It had come down to the wire, but I chose the job of Associate Engineer at Douglas, starting at $490 per month. It was November, 1960 and finally, rather than being grossly under employed, earning $52.50 per week (I had gotten a raise), I was now a real person with a real job. I could now make real plans for the future. It was as though I had died and gone to heaven.

Falling in love with Dolores had not only cranked up my ambition, but it made me feel that I was finally on the way to achieving unlimited success. After a month on the Douglas job, I asked Dolores to marry me. She said yes.

That Thanksgiving, Dolores and I decided to get together with the Greens to have dinner. We arrived early in the morning. John and I decided to go out and find a turkey. The first store we went to had fresh turkeys for about sixty-five cents a pound. We huffed at the storekeeper and marched out of the store to find a better deal. We found a better deal at one of the big chain food stores. We grabbed a twenty pound, thirty cents per pound, rock solid, frozen turkey and rushed back to the house. We were so proud of ourselves for having avoided being ripped off. The women started cooking around 11 AM. The big issue soon became how we were going to thaw the damned turkey. We all worked and worked on that sucker. Finally, we threw the turkey in the oven. It cooked and cooked until about 8 PM, when we all gave up. The four of us decided to eat the turkey anyway. Even though there were still some uncooked spots, we finally had our Thanksgiving dinner.

In the spring of 1961, Dolores and I got married in a little Methodist Church on Adams Boulevard, called Holman Memorial. John and Pat Green were the Best Man and Matron of Honor respectively. After a small reception at my Granddad's home in Venice, Dolores and I slipped away for a brief weekend honeymoon at a small motel on Washington Boulevard in LA. Then it was back to work. We moved into a two-unit apartment that Granddad had built in his backyard at 659 Vernon in Venice. This was the same place I had lived when I was seven-years-old. I had come full circle.

Dolores and I were starting down the road of life together. It seemed like it was going to be all down hill from here. We started down the path of an intense, five-year marriage that produced two lovely daughters. Unfortunately, it ended in divorce.

As it turned out though, my life was still just beginning. My career struggles and the quest for a middle class existence is another story for another time.

The End

About the Author

"Rich White Folks" is the personal memoir of **Robert H. Randolph**, a former Senior International Computer Industry Marketing Consultant. Having retired after forty years in corporate America, he reflects on what it was like growing up Black in America in the 1940's and '50's. Starting with his slave grandfather's story, he chronicles his life beginning with being born in Dallas, Texas, to his mother kidnapping him to Los Angeles. We follow his odyssey from Los Angeles to living in the Missouri Ozarks by the age of seven.

He takes us from being educated in a one-room school to his personal triumph of graduating from the University of Missouri at Kansas City, with a degree in Mathematics. His story is at times funny, at other times moving, and often educational. You will learn the origin of that phrase, "rich white folks" that served as a guidepost during his quest for the middle class American dream.

Mr. Randolph currently resides on the outskirts of Boston, Massachusetts.

CPSIA information can be obtained at www.ICGtesting.com
Printed in the USA
BVOW03s1729230914

367980BV00008B/126/P